Angel Day,

The English Secretary, and the Seventeenth Earl of Oxford

A new study by

Robert Sean Brazil

Angel Day, The English Secretary,
and the Seventeenth Earl of Oxford

by Robert Sean Brazil

First published 2013 by
Cortical Output LLC, Seattle, WA 98103, USA

ISBN 978-0-9853938-1-6

Contents

CHAPTER ONE

Rediscovering the place of *The English Secretary* in English literature

IN 16TH-CENTURY ENGLAND, the arts of rhetoric and, in particular, letter writing, grew to wide popular interest, driven by the rapidly changing social hierarchy and the precise needs of commerce and politics. Several early English books introduced cultured readers to the fine formulas of courtesy in communications, though these relied on translations from classical authors. Humanist writers, like Erasmus, taught the formal rules of writing as one path to an improved, more civil and educated society. But the appearance in 1586 of an ornate publication by the previously unknown Angel Day was something entirely new, titled, *The ENGLISH Secretorie wherein is contayned A PERFECT METHOD for the inditing of all manner of Epistles and familiar letters, together with their diversities, enlarged by examples under their severall Tytles. In which is layd forth a Path-waye, so apt, plaine and easie, to any learners capacity, as the like wherof hath not at any time heretofore beene delivered. Nowe first devized, and newly published by ANGEL DAYE. Altior fortuna Virtus.*

This book is now largely forgotten, save for a few scholars of the history of communications, or rhetoric, or Renaissance letter writing. But in 1586, The English Secretary became an instant bestseller, stayed in print for five decades, and was widely influential in its time.

Here follow a few extracts from modern-day mainstream scholars about The English Secretary. More complete analysis regarding the extant scholarship on Day's book appears later throughout this study.

> Angel Day's *English Secretary* was not only among the most popular letterwriters of its time, it was also the most ambitious. To begin with, Day's was the first English letterwriter **declaring itself to be comprised almost entirely of original letters.**

The link between secretaryship and secrecy was regularly asserted in the period, but perhaps never more saliently than by Angel Day, who insists repeatedly in his letterwriting manual *The English Secretary* that **a secretary is foremost 'a keeper or conserver of the secret unto him committed.**'

Richard Rambuss, "The Secretary's Study... " English Literary History 59 (1992)

Today the visual and oral has replaced, in part, the extraordinary power of the written word. Not so in the Renaissance. Then, idea movement was oral and written, the latter the medium for churchman, nobleman, or merchant. Thus there appeared in English a seminal work that tried to suggest theories, requirements, and examples of good written composition: Angell Day's *The English Secretary or Method of Writing Epistles and Letters.*

The letters for the most part are pragmatic, superior to the theory section which simply carries rhetoric over to letter writing.

One could hypothesize further that as more people left Latin for the vernacular, the common man had to incorporate the flowers of rhetoric into his communication when writing to persons of privilege: the merchant, politician, churchman, nobleman, master. **Ordinary writing, plain writing would remind the common man of his lower class. Would it not be to the writer's benefit to secure an aristocrat's approval by using similar devices that would sound agreeable? The many letters of Day seem to suggest just that.**

Herbert W. Hildebrandt, "A 16th Century Work on Communication: Precursor of Modern Business Communication," University of Michigan, 1979

Some of Day's sample letters are certainly modeled more on fiction than on life. For example, **the stylistic embellishments of his letters "descriptorie" and "laudatorie" suit them more to prose romance than to practical communication,** while the copious variations on themes like the love of learning to be found among the letters "hortatorie" turn them into moral essays rather than casual exchanges. ...Furthermore, **the circulation in Day of a wide-ranging repertoire of social interaction scripts would certainly have been an invaluable resource for dramatists, like Shakespeare, who sought to simulate the situated discourse of people of all ranks.**

Lynne Magnusson, *Shakespeare and Social Dialogue: Dramatic language and Elizabethan Letters*, Cambridge University Press, 1999.

Books like *The English Secretary* surely found their places on many a writing table... It can be ascertained that Shakespeare, for one, learned his lessons well. An examination of Day's figures will quickly reveal that, while he speaks of them as ornaments, they are sufficiently comprehensive to include ... almost all the realm of rhetoric. But **Shakespeare does more than use the figures as ornamentation to beautify his works,** ...he employed the figures functionally to emphasize the development of plot and character. It seems to me likely that he did not rely entirely on his memory of his grammar school training for the information he needed. **There is at least a strong likelihood that he kept some manual beside him, and as Day's is in certain respects the best and most popular it may very well have been**

the book he used. More than that we cannot at present speculate.

Robert O. Evans [Professor Emeritus in English at the University of Kentucky in the introduction to his 1966 reprint of the 1599 version of *The English Secretary.*

Magnusson and Evans both tiptoe into suggesting that ***Shakespeare*** was influenced by Day's examples of social letters in *The English Secretary.* This is significant, considering the wide-ranging use by Shakespeare of letters in his plays, never gratuitous, but always adding specific humor, condensing action through first-person accounts read aloud, and moving the plot along, often causing unexpected twists.

Letters in Shakespeare

Consider for a minute the crucial role that penned letters of communication play in the Shakespeare dramas: from the comedic forged letter of *Twelfth Night* to the intercepted letters in *Hamlet* and *Romeo and Juliet* that become matters of life and death.

A letter may go where a person may not; both up and down the social scale. Wax-sealed letters were the only form of communication-at-a-distance that could be trusted. Yet that trust was always on shaky grounds as carriers could be abducted or robbed and private matters disclosed. Additionally, there was always the problem of completely false letters (written by someone other than the alleged sender) or authentic letters that contained deceitful or misleading news. A bald lie, not believed when tendered in person, might be floated in a letter and buy a person more time. Shakespeare uses letters as miniature narratives to relate far-away, offstage actions in a manner more credible and efficient than narration by a superfluous character or chorus. Often, Shakespeare's fictional letters are the means of misdirection or mischief.

Alan Stewart, in *Shakespeare's Letters,* 2008, counts no less than one-hundred-and-eleven letters interspersed in the plays. He finds only five plays (out of 37) that don't employ letters to move the plot along.

Martin Scofield, in an article in Shakespeare Survey 51 (1998) summarizes some of Shakespeare's best- known dramatic applications of letters (sent and received).

...letters in Shakespeare are more often than not extremely untrustworthy or at least problematic—either because they are intended to trick or deceive, or because they are self-deceiving, or because they give bad advice or advice which the recipient is unwilling to take. ...Don Armado to Jaquenetta in *Love's Labour's Lost...* Orlando in *As You Like It* ... the Duke intercepts Valentine's letter in *Two Gentlemen of Verona* ... The letter in 2.4 of *1Henry IV* which warns Hotspur against his undertaking against the King is condemned as that of a "frosty spirited rogue" ... The letters to Brutus as if coming from Rome itself ... The letter of Cressida to

> Troilus in Act 5 comes after Troilus has seen Cressida's infidelity with Diomedes as "Words, words, mere words, no matter from the heart." ...Edmund's forged letter in *King Lear* brings about Edgar's alienation from his father ... Goneril's to Edmund, intercepted by Edgar, reveals a further dimension of her corruption... Letters are also vulnerable to delay (a turning point in the tragedy of *Romeo and Juliet* ... destruction (as in Julia's tearing up of Proteus' latter in the *Two Gentlemen of Verona*) and **ambiguity of author or addressee** (as in Valentine's writing a letter as if from Julia, which she then gives to him, in the same play). ... **In short, letters in Shakespeare's plays are distinctly slippery and malleable entities, more often the cause of misunderstandings and failures of communication than pure or ardent or displaying the force of friendship.**

If Shakespeare's dramatic letters employ the arts and crafts of rhetoric for good or ill, what sort of inspiration did he draw from Day's manual?

There is more to *The English Secretary* than meets the eye. Hidden qualities, seen especially in the 1586 first quarto, involve the bold humor in the example letters and a specificity of detail that was dropped, bit by bit, in the successive editions that Day re-edited. And, even though parts of the original were excised in later versions, dozens of new example letters and three new expository sections were added for the 1592/93 edition that remained in the package ever after. These new letters, allegedly more circumspect, in fact contain much deeply amusing material. Yet, as we shall see, there was nothing at all "funny" or "humorous" about Angel Day. He was a very serious scrivener devoid of any apparent natural wit. The Byzantine aristocratic wit that shines through the peculiar letters in his book is entirely out of synch with his otherwise reticent and apologetic personality. Angel Day is a paradox wrapped in duplicity.

The mixed message of *The English Secretary* was noticed early on. The otherwise obscure John Massinger (no known relation to playwright Philip Massinger), published, in 1640, *The Secretary in Fashion*. This was essentially a translation of a French book of that same year, *Secretarie a la mode*, by Jean Puget de le Serre. But in the preface, Massinger states that he hopes his book will finally supplant Day's book, which was still popular in 1640 (54 years after the first edition) and still available to another new generation via *The English Secretary*'s 1635 printing. Massinger wrote that he hoped to "reclaim the idolatrous from adoring that **malicious idol**, *The English Secretary*." Massinger also warned that anyone who did not heed his advice to purchase and venerate his *Secretary in Fashion* would be "condemned to the reading of *The English Secretary* as long as thou livest."

Why did he consider *The English Secretary* a malicious idol? Simply because the book was still selling well and provided tough competition? Or because, at the very brink of the English Civil Wars (usually dated at 1642-1661, and fought in three acts, like a modern play) there was a great sensitivity to anything possibly sneaky, cheeky, or dangerous to church and state. While this assessment assumes Massinger's sincerity in his harsh statement, no other contemporary or modern commentator has called Day's *Secretary* malicious or an unrightfully venerated object of idolatrous fools.

There are several fascinating omissions in almost all the extant scholarship on Angel Day and *The English Secretary*. One is the depth of humor, absurdity, and digression in many of Day's example letters, all in direct contradiction to his espoused principles of brevity, truthfulness, and aptness. The second involves Day's documented relationship to the 17th Earl of Oxford. For over a century, all commentators on Day managed to erase the fact that Angel Day was engaged in at least some secretarial service to the Earl of Oxford during the 1580s-'90s, and that ***all*** editions of his book, from the first in 1586 to the rest, begin with dedications to Oxford. Only the most recent commentators (J. R. Henderson, in *British Rhetoricians and Logicians 1500-1660* [DLB, vol. 236, 2001] and L. Magnusson, in *Shakespeare and Social Dialogue: Dramatic language and Elizabethan Letters*, Cambridge University Press, 1999) have shown fit to acknowledge that Oxford was a dedicatee of Day's work. Nevertheless, all scholars on Day (*including* these two who admit Oxford's presence in the story) never classify Oxford as Day's actual employer. Nor do they consider that it was precisely in this documented time frame (1586 to 1599), while under Oxford's patronage, that Angel Day honed his craft and *published all his known works.* From what Day says about the especially close bond between a lord and his secretary, and the importance of discretion and the keeping of the master's secrets, and Day's own statements in the updated dedications to Oxford, there can be little question of Angel Day's service to de Vere and his household. Though direct external corroboration is lacking (like pay chits), the dates of the editions and updated dedications give us a window of Day's tenure with Oxford. Already on terms with Oxford in 1586, Day was still in service to the earl in 1592/93, 1595, and 1599, as evidenced by the updated dedications to Oxford in each of the later editions of *The English Secretary*. All scholars agree that Day's work on the project ceased after 1599; that popular edition was the one that was subsequently duplicated, in many more printings, through 1635.

Secretary, take a letter

In the present, 21st century, when we hear the quaint word, "secretary," the first thing that may come to mind is an office secretary of the 1950s or '60s. Her hair is up in a bun; she is typing, smoking, and watching the clock. Such a secretary took dictation or retyped notes for office correspondence. She might have had to pick up lunch for he boss. He may have had additional requests. With such associations (valid or not) the term "secretary" has become almost demeaning, an anachronism like "stewardess" or "shoe-shine boy." Yesterday's office secretaries are now executive assistants. Yet we also have the respected terms, Secretary of State, Secretary of Defense, and Secretary of the Treasury, etc., all important cabinet positions in the USA with similarly-named counterparts in most other countries. No one would confuse a secretary with a Secretary. At the time of the final revision of *The English Secretary* in 1599, Robert Cecil was titled the "Secretary of State" for England, the first with that precise title. He rose to the position after the death of Walsingham, whose title had been "Principal Secretary."

The term "secretary" had been in use in English, in both senses, before the 16th century. But it can be easily argued that the many editions of Day's *English Secretary* popularized the word, and the office. It was the first book in English with "Secretary" in the title. To Angel Day, a secretary was not just a master of letters but also the trusted keeper of his employer's secrets. A *Secret*-ary. In a sense, high-level political Secretaries are more in the business of keeping secrets than demonstrating a mastership of rhetoric and style.

In this study I will propose one reason why Day's book has fallen off the radar. Some scholars of the period think that Shakespeare was very much indebted to Angel Day, and may have had his *English Secretary* open on his desk while writing. This stylistic links between Day's example letters and Shakespeare's fictional ones might be more exploited if there wasn't the inconvenience of Edward de Vere looming so prominently in the picture. There is so much overlap in language and style between the example letters in *The English Secretary* and Oxford's dozens of extant business letters to William and Robert Cecil that one must flirt with the conclusion that the Earl provided the humorous example letters that pepper the book throughout.

While Professor Evans tentatively suggests that Shakespeare learned rhetorical ornamentation from Day, and Magnusson posits that he learned the parsing of social interaction and courtesy there, I suggest that the influence is found in the cunning, explicit humor of *The English Secretary*'s examples. Further, the influence will eventually be recognized to have been the other way around, with the same veiled author who penned the plays (that became known as Shakespeare's) contributing the peculiar letters that filled out Day's letter-writing manual.

¶ To the right Honourable Lord, *EDWARD de VERE, Earle of* Oxenford, Viſcount Bulbeck, Lord Sandford *and of Badeleſmere, and Lord great Camberlaine of England,* all Honour and happineſſe, correſpondent to his moſt Noble deſires, and in the commutation of this earthlie beeing, endleſſe ioyes and an euerlaſting habitation.

EVXES endeuouring to paint excellentlie, made Grapes in ſhewe ſo naturall, that preſenting thē to view men were deceaued with their ſhapes and the birdes with their cullours. When Apelles *drew* Venus *(though the ſhew of bewtie ſeemed woonderful) he daunted not in his workmanſhip, becauſe he knew his cunning excellent.*

If

CHAPTER TWO

The link to Oxford through the dedication

THE OBVIOUS AND immediate link from Angel Day to the Earl of Oxford is through the dedication at the front of every edition of *The English Secretary.*

The 1586 dedication reads:

> To the right honourable Lord, EDWARD de VERE, Earl of Oxenford, Viscount Bulbeck, Lord Sandford and of Badlesmere, and Lord great Camberlaine of England, all Honour and happinesse, correspondent to his most Noble desires, and in the commutation of this earthly beeing, endless joyes and an everlasting habitation.
>
> ZEUXES endevouring to paint excellent lie, made Grapes in shewe so naturall, *that presenting them to view men were deceaved with their shapes and the birdes with their cullours. When Apelles drew Venus (though the shew of bewtie seemed woonderful) he daunted not in his workmanship, because he knew his cunning excellent.*
>
> *If in penning I were as skilful as the least of these in painting: I should neither faint to present a discourse to Alexander, nor to tell a tale to a Philosopher.*
>
> *My honourable L. the exceeding bountie wherewith your good L. hath ever wonted to entertaine the desertes of all men, and very apparaunce of Nobility her selfe, wel known to have reposed her delights in the worthines of your stately mind warranteth me: almost, that I need not blush to recommend unto your curteous vew, the first fruits of these my formost labours, and to honour this present discourse with the memorie of your everlasting worthinesse. And albeit by the learned view and insight of your L. whose infancy from the beginning was ever sacred to the Muses, the whole course heereof may be found nothing suche, as in the lowest part of the same may appeare in any sort answerable to so greate and forward excellence: and that the continuaunce of this slender substance, is in no point matchable to manie thinges of greater science, passing under your honourable countenaunce: yet may your L. please to consider, that presentes (not out of the riche store and plentye a lone of the wealthiest) are alwaies receiued as testimonies of regarde, in*

the reputation of the mightiest: but sometimes trifles also ensuing of lesse habilitie, (not honoured or reputed of by theyr valew, but by the generous estate and surpassing bountie of the receiuer) are accompted of, moste especially.

For the shrowd of my defence, that have so much dared upon presumption of your accustomed fauor, to infixe your honoured name in the forefronte of this my traueile: I can propoze no one in example unto your L. more worthie then your selfe, who not unacquainted with the speciall partes and aeternized memorie of them all, have long since endevoured your self to become a noble patterne of them all, the exemplifieng of whose praise, cannot by anie speeches of mine, be herein more greatlye put forwardes, then the same long since hath bene published by the renowme of your own proper vertues.

My humble request unto your L. is, that your gentle acceptance hereof may be an encouragement to my after endevours, for whose sake I knowe the same shalbe of many regarded, and the insufficiency thereof the better protected. In which, besides the continuall manifestation of your owne worthinesse, your L. shall binde me to honor you in al duetie and humblenes, praying the eternall creator and guid of all your stately enterprises, to have the same with your L. in his favorable protection.

Your L. most devoted and loyally affected.

Angel Daie.

We must note immediately the association of the 17th Earl of Oxford with these specific names evoking specific stories of the classical era: 1) Zeuxis; 2) Apelles; 3) Venus; 4) Alexander. These four relate dynamically with the Shakespearean writings, to Oxford's poems, and to other dedications to de Vere. A full discussion of this is found in Chapter 13.

In brief, Zeuxis was a Greek master artist whose painted grapes tempted real birds. The anecdote appears in the Shakespeare poem, *Venus and Adonis.* Apelles, another Grecian painter, modeled a painting of Venus on the beautiful lady friend of Alexander the Great, Campaspe (Pancaspe).

Note also what Day says about Oxford in 1586:

> My honourable L. the exceeding bountie wherewith your good L. hath ever wonted to entertaine the desertes of all men …

The exceeding bounty (generosity) of Oxford's personality has "ever wonted to entertaine the desertes of all men". This could either mean that Oxford had been helpful at furthering men's careers, or more simply, that he has provided bountiful entertainment to all.

> "… by the learned view and insight of your L. whose infancy from the beginning was ever sacred to the Muses …

"Ever sacred to the muses" means only one thing in this context: Oxford was a master poet, versifier, tale-teller, songwriter, and dramatic artist. He has the skills and qualities of Apollo.

> For the shrowd of my defence, that have so much dared upon presumption of your accustomed favor, to infixe your honoured name in the forefronte of this my traveile

"Presumption of your accustomed favor"—either Day was already accustomed to some favor from Oxford or he is referring to others who dedicated books to Oxford and were, presumably, rewarded.

> My humble request unto your L. is, that **your gentle acceptance hereof may be an encouragement to my after endevours,** for whose sake I knowe the same shal be of many regarded and the insufficiency thereof the better protected. In which, besides the continuall manifestation of your owne worthinesse, **your L. shall binde me to honor you in al duetie and humblenes,** praying the eternall creator and guid of all your stately enterprises, to have the same with your L. in his favorable protection.
>
> **Your L. most devoted and loyally** affected.

Whether Day was or was not in a formal or informal employment with Oxford before 1586, he is here clearly stating his readiness for the task. Day tells Oxford that his acceptance will encourage Day to write more, and feel "better protected." He requests that Oxford bind him to honor, and declares devotion and loyalty. While some of this language may be attributed to "boilerplate" Elizabethan sincerity and supplication, in my view, Day was already in Oxford's service at the time he began assembling and writing his book.

CHAPTER THREE

A look at the letters

BEFORE GETTING TOO DEEP in the analysis, it is important to appreciate the flavor of the unique example letters in *The English Secretary*. At this point we will stick to the 1586 first edition. This version contains 52 demonstrative letters, seven "love letters," and one faux-epistle yielding a total of 60 examples.

Here is the beginning of the first example Day gives, on how not to write an epistle. In this section I have modernized the spelling where possible to ease comprehension. In a supplemental chapter I reprint example letters in original spelling. The example is a proposed preface to a book of medicine:

> Egregious Doctors, and masters of the eximious & Arcane Science of Phisick, of your urbanity exasperate not yourselves against me, for making of this little volume of Phisick. Considering that my pretence is for an utilitie and a commonwealth. And this not onely, but also I do it for no detriment, but for a preferment of your lawdable science, that everie man shoulde esteem, repute and regard the excellent facultie. And also you to bee extolled and highly preferred, that hath and doth studie, practise and labour this said Arcane science, to the which none inartious persons, can nor shall attain to the knowledge: yet notwithstanding fools and insipient persons, yea and manie the which, doth thinke themselves wise (the which in this facultie be fooles in deed) will enterprise.

In this short example we find several of Oxford's distinctive or habitual words and phrases, "against me"—"considering that"—"pretence"—"not only, but also"—"detriment"—"but for"—"esteem"—"regard"—"excellent"—"labour"—"the which"—"notwithstanding"—"enterprise."

In this example, the writer explains to his wife where he has been and why she should not worry about him:

I Doubt not, N. but that thy heart longeth, and mind is yet unquieted, because of my sodden departure from thee, and ignorance of my estate and present being, whereof that thy desires may now at full be resolved: know my good N. that not having been scarce sixe months from thee, I did long since perceive myself to be out of England, and that it may appear unto thee, that I have juste cause so to say, thou shalt somewhat understand by me the state of this Country. We live heere in a soil, delicate I must confesse for the air, and pleasant for the situation with good leisure I must tell thee may we here attend our devotions, as having no cares wherewith to encomber us, but the needless search of that whereof we never finde likelihoode to annoy us. As uncompelled by severe decrees and interdictions we limit unto ourselves an abstinence, thou mightest think we do it of zeale, but in truth it is of want, wherein we have more fasting daies by a great many then ability to beare them. Our conversation is with elementes, with waters, with fields, with trees, with valleys, with hills, in the general use whereof we finde nothing else but their proper shapes. And if by chance any other sorts of creatures do appear, they are naked shapes formed as men and wemen, fierce, savage, wilde, not capable of any our reasons, nor we of their speaches. Our food is rootes, dried fishes, berries, and I know not what other harsh kinde of fruites, and sometimes fowls, besides a kinde of grain growinge in great cods, whereby we sometimes obtaine (though not the naturall) yet some use of bread, unlike to that you eate, in taste, goodnesse or property. Our lodgings and places of repose are caves, entrenched in the ground, the earth our beds, and cloaths our coveringes. And these also hard as they are, enioy we not in quiet, but being awaited of the naked multitude (whose policies insinuate by nature are far greater then their strength) we are faine by much industry to prevent them: into whose handes if any of us do chance to fall, our dead carcasses in hasty morsels are conveyed into their entrailes. Hereby judginge of our estate, thou mayest accordingly deem of our pleasures. The next message that thou shalt attende from me, shall be my speedy returne, the Seas and winds being not lesse favourable then they were at my going foorth. Meanwhile recommending my self to thy well wishing, and our safeties to God. I ende as thou knowest this of, &c.

Comments:

1. If you did not find this funny the first time through, try reading it in a voice like John Cleese, or Peter Sellers.

2. Oxford's wife Anne, would be, familiarly, "Nan" as his Edward would be "Ned." Annes and Edwards often become Nan and Ned in the Shakespeare plays. The letter is written to N. after a sudden overseas escape and tries to make light of the abandonment with an incredulous tale of provincial hardship. Oxford was in just this position several times and may have written such a letter home. I'm not suggesting for a minute that this is the letter, only that it is suggestive of what his personal letters (which have all vanished) might look like.

3. The description of this strange country and the harsh foods available there is very similar to the descriptions of flora and fauna found on Prospero and Caliban's isle in *The Tempest.*

English Secretary		Our food is **rootes**, dried **fishes**, **berries**, and I know not what other harsh kinde of fruites, and sometimes fowls, besides a **kinde of grai**n growinge in great cods.
Tempest	Prospero	… thy food shall be the fresh-brook mussels, **wither'd roots,** and **husks** wherein the acorn cradled. …
	Caliban	I'll show thee the best springs; I'll pluck thee **berries**; I'll **fish** for thee.
English Secretary		Our **lodgings and places of repose are caves, entrenched in the ground**, the earth our beds, and cloaths our coveringes.
Tempest	Prospero	Welcome, sir; this cell's my court; here have I few attendants, and subjects none. …
	Prospero	Sir, I invite your Highness and your train to my poor cell, where you shall take your rest.
English Secretary		And if by chance any other sorts of creatures do appear, they are naked shapes formed as men and wemen, fierce, **savage,** wilde, **not capable of any our reasons, nor we of their speaches**.
Tempest	Miranda	(to Caliban) "Abhorred slave, which any print of goodness wilt not take, being **capable of all ill**! I pitied thee, Took pains to make thee speak, taught thee each hour one thing or other. When **thou didst not, savage, know thine own meaning, but wouldst gabble like a thing most brutish**..."
English Secretary		… shall be my speedy returne, the Seas and winds being not lesse favourable then they were at my going fFoorth.
Tempest	Prospero	I'll deliver all; and promise you calm seas, auspicious gales, and sail so expeditious.
English Secretary		… a soil, delicate I must confesse for the air, and pleasant …
Tempest	Gonzalo	How lush and lusty the grass looks! how green! …
	Adrian	The air breathes upon us here most sweetly.
English Secretary		Our conversation is with elementes, with waters, with fields, with trees, with valleys, with hills.
Tempest	Caliban	all the qualities o' th' isle, The fresh springs, brine-pits, barren place and fertile. …
	Prospero	Ye elves of hills, brooks, standing lakes, and groves …

Here's an example from *The English Secretary* that recommends how a son might respond to a coldhearted father. Keep in mind that this is supposed to be a serious recommendation of clarity and brevity and sincere supplication.

> **If floods of tears sealed with hard and bitter sighs**, if continual sorrow and never ceasing care, if consuming griefs not of a diseased body, but of a pestered mind, might have rendered sufficient and assured testimony, whereby to persuade your

> laden ears surcharged by this time with the weight of my incessant and continual cries: the intolerable woes wherein I live, secluded from the right and name of a son, and barred quite from the sweet and gentle term of a loving and kind father, had ere this time given mean of recovery to my daunted and dismayed spirits, and kindled in me some wan hope, one day to have found an hour so happy, wherein by a right conceit conceived of my unkindly pleasures, or convinced by the importunitie of those who have pittied my evils, your naturall care might in some sorte or other have beene renewed, to the redress of all my forewearied and heavie groning mischiefs.

That's just one sentence. Oxford also wrote perilously long sentences and used the repeated "If…" motif. Several of his poems begin this way: "If care or skill could conquer vain desire"—"If women could be fair and yet not fond." Oxford also uses the metaphor "flood of tears" in a poem:

> And Caesar that presented was, with noble Pompey's princely head
> As 'twere some judge to rule the case, a flood of tears he seemed to shed

Oxford also uses—almost as a signature—hard, bitter, sighs, sorrow, griefs, etc.:

> Who taught thee first to **sigh**, alas, my heart?
> Who taught thy tongue the **woe**ful words of plaint? [love]
> Who filled thine eyes with **tears** of **bitter** smart?
> Who gave thee **grief** and made thy joys so faint?

We also find recovery:

> Framed in the front of forlorn hope, past all recovery …

And happy hour:

> I hover high and soar where hope doth tower,
> Yet froward fate defers my happy hour.

The English Secretary letter continues:

> … the hateful show of my ill deserts, is yet become of so loathed and detestable recordation, in this very season unto you: then (as before time I eftsoones have done) I do confess my letters untimely also at this instant to have approached unto you.

Oxford:

> …you will let him have his deserts according to his presumption…

> …one Luke Atslow that served—who is now become a lewd subiect to Her Majesty and an evil member to his country.

Master Frobisher hath already very honourably attempted, and is now eftsoons to be employed for the better...

...desiring your (honour) that at this instant as heretofore you have given me your good word...

Vocabulary aside, one has to wonder, if Day wrote the letters himself, where did he develop the imagination to write such vividly overwrought examples that make a mockery out of his careful explanations and deconstructions of how an appropriate letter should flow?

This example letter from *The English Secretary* 1586 recommends the hiring of a most unsuitable servant:

Sir I do send unto your view the bearer hereof (a man shaped as you see, and as bold in condition as he appeareth in show) whome by all the superfluities of summer ale, that hath wrought in his giddy brain, I have been requested to commend unto you. And inasmuch as in putting forward so unworthy a worthy, in substance of so incredible allowance, it something behooveth I hide not the single gifts which by great search in many a good Hostrie, Taverne, and Alehouse, he hath by long travail and drowsy experience ere this time gained, to his insupportable credence, I shall not spare in some sort to signify unto you, what in regard of all these I am led to conjecture. Truth is Sir that he is very well studied in the mystery of malt-worms, and for his peculiar skill in decerning the nappy taste by the nutbrowne collor of celler ale in a frosty morning, he is become a sworn brother of the ragmans number, and thereby standeth enjoined never to wear furs or other lining in the coldest winter, but onely the warmth of the good ale which inwardly must harten him: besides Sir, if you have occasion to credit him with a small parcel of money in dispatch of a journey, do but say the word, that it shall once lie in his charge, and you may stand assured, that it shall be laid up so safe, as any liquor in the world can safe conduct it from his belly. Take no care for your kitchen, buttery, or larder, for once a day he loves to see all clean before him, little apparel will serve him, for his liveries ensue weekely, out of the brewers meshfat. His lodging he wrecks not, the chimney store, and billets ends serve for fetherbed and coverings. When you have moste neede of him, you shall alwaies be sure to goe without him: if you delight in a pigs-nie, you may by receiving of him, become sure of a hogshead. Great store of small liking you happily may have to him, we know not what wonders the worle may rend out, for nothing is impossible where al; thinges may be compassed. It may please you for recreations sake to look upon him so you be not in case to surfeit, look what ill liking you conceive, report back again I pray you in the inner facing of his chimney casket, Omnia sua secum portat he is somewhat a foolosopher, for he carries his possessions about him, for terram dedit filijs hominum, he must needes then have a large dwelling. I pray sir, give him good words how ill favoredly soever you favour his acquaintance. For my part I request no remuneration for the preferment, I have tendered towards him.

Thus much would I have done & more long since to be rid of him. His old master being dead it is necessary some place to be pestered with him, he makes great choice of your housekeeping, if you can like to frame with him. Much more might be delivered in the condemnation of his worthinesse, but that I leave to rehearse it,

> but now Sir, for your own appetite I leave to your contentment: Blame not me, but him that led me, and so forth to an end. Commend mee, but not condemn me, for I shall once doe you a better turne, this is but the first, the next may be worse (better) I would say. And so fare yee well, &c

It is nigh impossible to imagine Day creating this marvelous character sketch of a useless drunk.

The Latin phrase, "*Omnia sua secum portat*" is a shortening of the motto "*Sapiens Omnia sua secum portat*" A wise man takes everything he owns with him. This man has nothing, but brings it along. He is not wise.

Terram dedit filijs hominum—This Latin phrase is from Psalm 115, line 16: [The heavens are the Lord's heavens] but *the earth he has given to the children of man*: Literally: He gave the land to the sons of men.

This next letter is darkly comic. The pretense is that we are being instructed in the proper manner by which a mother may be informed and consoled over the loss of her son. In this example I have modernized the spelling and abridged the length.

> **Good Mistresse P.** I am sorry that my self must become the unlucky messenger of mine own infortunity unto you, & that in the forefront of my letter is planted such extreme grief, as I cannot but extreemly bewayle, so often as I think of it.—But what shall I rehearse unto you a thing so sudden and unlooked for, as I protest by the heavenly maker and ruler of all things, at the receipt of your last letters I never mistrusted, or once looked for to have happened? Your tears I see, even now await what I will say, and lo, your imaginations do already deem the matter I must utter.—It is then your son, good M. P. whose want I am forced to tolerate, and whose presence you must now hencefoorth determine utterly to forbear. Your last presage in commanding him to be seen living or dead, hath now returned his living to be discharged, and his earthly course unlooked for, to be covered with cinders.—He is commaunded to an other, that before did expect him, he is swallowed in the gulf, that from the foremost hour of his birth did hitherto await him.
>
> Now if you will say he was young and might have lived, examples do show that younger than he have died. If you will say you loved him greatly: God by your patience shall accept him the more worthily. If you will say you are sorry for it, in that he was virtuous: consider the world wherein he lived, that might have made him more vicious.—Know ye not, that all thinges do by little and little grow unto ripeness and forthwith by degrees they fall unto rottenness? Hath not God and nature unto everie thing after their greatest perfection, included such certain limits, that by and by they seem adapted to their latest confusion?—Among all fruites and blossomes on the ground, are there not some that are sooner then others, even on their tenderest branches as it were already ripened, and others again that by long lying are made rotten and mellowed?
>
> To man also is appointed his certaine boundes, unto which to be attained, and beyond the which not to be exceeded, is already limited. Your sonne, as timely fruit,

so timely ripened, and as fit for his season was as timely gathered.—

If physic could have saved him, if syrups, hot potions, or other necessaries would have cured him, if tears and prayers might have kept him, you had yet hitherto in safety received him. He is dead, he is gone, and we must after him. Of his firste sickenesse he was whole and perfectlye recovered, afterwardes from the jaundice though somewhat weakened yet lastly delivered.—It is your part therefore to be now recomforted, and therein with patience to refer your self to God's determinate pleasure and judgement, to which intent I have taken in hand this midnight's labour, after the receipt of your letters, which were to be returned the next morning early, by reason whereof I can no ways satisfy what you write for, nevertheless resting hereafter to my utmost power to pleasure you, and recommending my selfe also to your wonted courtesy, I end this fourteenth of January, your carefull friend, &c.

No commentary is required on the above, beyond its complete inappropriateness in a manual of courtesy. What doubles the amazement is that *The English Secretary* letter writer tops himself a few pages after this one with a consolation letter to a new widow on the death of her husband. Again, I have trimmed the letter and modernized the spelling.

A Consolatorie Epistle of the third sorte, wherein a gentlewoman is comforted of the death of her husband slayn in the warres.

Albeit my self (having received the sorrowfull news of the untimely death of my dearest kinsman, and your deceased loving husband) was in the first hearing therof so greatly troubled with the heavy news, as by reason of the great griefe by me conceived in the same, my self happily might seem to need that comfort, which now I go about to bestow upon others: Yet weighing in my mind the state wherein you stand, and beeing also informed with what great extremitie you have entertained the newes of his losse, I cannot but in respect of the great love I ought to him, and remembrance of the like care, wherewith he principally favoured you, enforce my pen hereby to yield unto you those comfortable speeches by the veritie whereof my self in so great a storm of grief could hitherto as yet be verie hardly satisfied.—

Assuredly my good cousin, I must needs conclude with your owne speechs, and the weight of your interchaungeable likings, that there is great cause left unto you to become sorrowfull, as having lost the chief and principall iewell of all your worldly love and liking, the fauored companion of all your pleasaunt and youthfull yeares, the entire comfort and solace of your present happinesse, and suche a one, who above all worldes, or any earthly estimation at all, accompted, honoured, and entirelie more then anie others received and loved you: but that you have so great and vrgent cause of extremity to continue, with so hard impatience as you do, it befitteth not, it is unnecessarie, yea it is in my iudgement of al others the most insufferable.

For when it is not denied unto you, that you have cause to mourn, it is not fittest unto the matter of your love, to weep over him and to bewaile him, it is then thereby intended that there must be a meane therein, that the force thereof must bee limitted, that the apparaunce beare shewe of discretion. Doe we not all know I pray you, and are witnesses, that he was a mortall man, as our selues hee was borne under the same condition, that hee must once die, that he had his time set, beyond whiche hee might not passe, and that God who gaue him life thus long to live with you, hath now called him again, from this earth to leaue you?

Are we ignoraunt, that nature compelleth the wife for her husband, the husband for his wife, parentes for their children, and kindered for their kinsfolke, to weepe and lament? but followeth it not also therewith, that the losse and want of them being layd downe by an immooueable necessity; we can by no meanes afterwardes be in hope to reclaime them? **what great folly do we then commit in thus serching after the ghosts of our deceased frends?** or what other thing do we therein performe, but yeeld a plaine demonstration, that our teares are to none other end, but to bewayl them, because they were mortal? whom death could never have shunned, without they had bin immortall. **Are we not eftsoones put in minde by the common casualty of all things, that there is nothing stable, that daily and hourly kingdomes decay, provinces are shaken, countries destroyed, cities burned, towns wasted, people consumed, and that it remaineth a thing so ordinary with us, daily to be conversant in these evils) the losse of all, or other of which (if they may be accounted evils) why then doe we give our selves by unmeasurable griefe, to a perpetual continuance and renovation of those evils.**

But you will hereunto alleage, that it is love that inforceth you unto the same, and that such is the continual remembrance you have, as you cannot forget him. Alas, how fruitless is this love, and zealous remembrance in the deliveraunce thereof? Howe far sequestred is the vehemency of the same, from the searched recompence? Why learn we not rather of the wisest and worthiest, how to mitigate the impatience of our own imperfections?

In whose precepts, examples and counsels, if the immoderate use or entertainment of any thing be forbidden, shall we not then in this, above all others be chiefly reprehended, when we enforce our selves by continual meditation of our losses to shed so many tears to no purpose: what if your husband had not now died, at this instant, he must you knowe have died, he could not always have lived, yea but he died you say untimely, what call you untimely I pray you? If in respect of the force prevayling upon him, wherby he was slaine, you name it untimely, then do I graunt unto it.

But if in regarde of the time of his life you affirme it, I denie that the same may then be said untimely. For why? hath not the eternall creator of all thinges ordered by his divine wisdom each matter to pass his course in sort to himself best beseeming and most pleasing? howe can you then say that to bee untimelie which by his heavenly moderation was so appointed? assure your selfe, if hee had then beene at home wyth you, he had also died, you could not have prevented it his houre was come, so was it determined, which way could she shunne it.

What then greeueth you in this action? is it that he was slaine? Consider with your selfe it was in his princes service, his death was thereby the more honourable, for in so dying, he died as a man, as a souldier, as a gentleman. Yea but you shall

never you say see him more: true indeede, but what of that? is this deathe now greater then his absence before? yes forsoothe it is in deede, and why? because you had hope then to see him againe, which by this meanes is taken away, verie well. You did then while he was living recomfort your selfe with hope, content your selfe now with necessitie because it must needes be so, and you can no waies amend it. Is not this an ende sufficient to determine all sorrowes? If you weepe, lament, crie out, and become grieued, requisite were it the same shoulde returne to some end, that all your care, sorrow, griefe, lamentation, or what els should not appeare fruitelesse, that the intendment & determination therof shuld be to some special purpose. See you then, herein is no supplie, the effectes are berest, the end taken away. Bee not then so fond as to bedew that with your teares wherunto belongeth neither redresse, nor meane of recovery. Who is hee that woulde bee so mad, as crie out unto him of whome he might bee assured never to obtaine remedie? By cunning art beastes wee see thoughe they be most fierce are tamed, a meane is found wherewith to breake the marble, the Adament how hard soever it be, may be deuises bee mollified: Onely deathe is of such force as no waies can be convinced.

At the leastwise, if neither of these arguments might move you to supprese your exceeding sorrows you must finally consider that we are Christians, and by the benefit of this corporal death, do make exchange of an uncorrupted life, that the withdrawing us from this vile earthly bodie of clay and filth, is a commutation to a sacred, and heavenly progression, and that we have nothing lefe unto us, in all the travailes, cares, disquiets, and heavie turmoiles of this wearisome living whereof to rejoice us, but the expectation we have of happinesse and ever flourishing gladness. Suppose the ghost of your husband were here present to see you, in all this extremitie, what thinke you, would he say? how much disordered imagine you would he thinke you to be in your affections?

And were it not that so many costes hadde severed him both by land and seas, peraduenture wearied with your bitter outcries, in the conceited image, & shape of death, you might in apparance heere him, in these like speeches accusing & rebuking such your distemperate actions. And with breathing spirit to cry out unto you saying. What is it you go about? what meane you by teares to serche out for a thing so irrecuperable? Why torment you your youthfull yeares, with such unprofitable, or rather as I may cal it, desperate kind of mourninges? why with such uniust tomplaintes accuse you fortune, and so often do appeale death and destinie of so haynous trespace? Is it for that you envie my happy state, so soone transported from this untoward soyle, to a more prosperous felicity. Thus credite me, and in this sort (wer it possible he could speak unto you) would he accuse you, in which consideration, were there not iust cause think you (of such intemperance) why you should be greatly ashamed? Beleeve me good cosin, there is neither profite or liking at all, of this bitter continuaunce reaped, you have alreadie waded sufficiently in your teares, you have mourned for him in ernest love as beseemed a wife, it is nowe hie time you be after all this comforted. Thinke that the greatest storme is by necessitie at length overblowen, superfluity of coales encreaseth rather heate then flame, the ardencie of affection, with vehemencie sufficient maye be expressed, though not by extremitie inforced. What should I say unto you? you may not as other foolish creatures, that are neither governed by wit, nor ordered by discretion, make your selfe a spectacle to the world, but rather with such temperature (for even in this extremitie of sorrow, is also planted a rare paterne of modestie) seek in such maner to demean your selfe, as the lookers on may rather pittie you, by insight of your great discretion, then in this sort to torment your selfe by a needles supposition. Much more have I considered with my selfe, whereby to satisfie my grieued immaginations, wherewith being recomforted, and repozed in my secret thoughtes. I have deemed it necessarie hereby to imparte the same unto you; beseeching, that aswell in regard of your selfe, as the little pleasure your frendes have, to behold you in this strange kind of perplexity, you will en ioy the fruites thereof with suche sufficient contentment and satisfaction as very hartily I do wish unto you. And even so tendring my selfe in al thinges to your courteous and gentle usage, I doe heartily bid you farewell, S. this of &c.

Even these two consolation letters above are outdone by the next where a man is consoled over the loss of his wife. Some of this is surprisingly inappropriate, even to a jaded modern reader. You have been warned.

An Example Consolatorie, pleasantly written to one, who had buried his olde wife.

The posting news hitherward of the late decease of my good old mistresse, your wife, hath made me in the very going away of mine ague fit, to strain my self to greet you by these letters. In the inditing wherof I many times prayed in my thoughts that I were as readily delivered of this my *tercian* fever, as **your self are in mine opinion delivered & by such means rid of a hatefull and very foule encumbrance. I doubt not sir, but you do now take the matter heavily, being thereby disposed as you are of such an intolerable delight, as wherewith you were continually cloyed by the nightly embracements of so unwieldy a carcasse.** I have I must confess very seldom known you for any thing to mourn, neverthelesse if by such means you be happily constrained to change countenance, I have prepared a golden box wherein I mean to consecrate all the tears you shed for that accident, to ***Berecynthia*** the beldome of the Gods as a relique of your great kindship and courtesy.

Believe me T. I am sorry that mine ague had not left me, and that I were not now in London with thee, were it but to view thy looks and manlike behauiour, after so hard a bickering an encounter, as wherein thou was bearest a heart of gold so dainty as I promise thee to some grave sober fellow, might have become pretty conceited, and a verye sweete pigges knee.

Well T. if thou must needs loose her, *ferendum est quod mutari non possit*, be not sad I pray thee, we'll find out a better match wherewith to delight thee. Thou must consider that it is requisite that **all things should be done with indifferency, she hath left a thousand pound in goodes and a hundred marks a year unto thee, let that content thee, what though she was not married a month to thee, thou must be a patient man, her long continuaunce with so much wealth might peradventure have glutted thee.**

The Gods have become more favourable to thy yong yeares, then thy self doest consider of: Shee might I know have lived longer time for age, (for four score years old I grant is nothing) the woman also in very good plight too, by ***Saint Margerie:*** but what of that? wee must as I said before, beare with necessitie. I pray God thou beest not overcome with sorrowe, but thou maiest take it quietly. There be men in the world that are so carelesse of their fortune, and so verie fooles in their wishing, as they coulde content themselues greatly to be in the lyke predicament with thee, but thou I assure my selfe art of a cleane contrarie opinion, sweare no more good T. I am perswaded alone that it utterly discontenteth thee. But hearest thou? playe not the madde man for all that, I will rather comfort thee my selfe, then that thou shouldest die for sorrow.

One thing greatly misliketh me, I heard saye thou tookest an oath upon her death bed never to marry again? See how love may lead men? Good GOD it is strange? I promise thee I could hardly be persuaded thou did so, without I should hear thee sweare it. Be not so sottishe good boy, remember thy selfe, and thinke on the Philosophers wordes: ***Non nobis solum nati sumus.*** thou maiest **have a wife man, and become the father of ninety-nine children perchance ere thou die.**

Forsweare thou nothing good T. but building of monasteries and entring into religion, for these my selfe dare undertake thou never wilt nor mentest to do. I would faine talk longer with thee but I am wearie, & therfore intend to leaue the expectation of the rest, till I fortune to see thee. Fare (as otherwise **thou canst not choose**) well, having neither old wife nor fever, wherewith to encomber thee. At S. this of &c.

Notes

tercian fever

Tercian fever is a medieval term. Chaucer speaks of *tercian fever.* It is now spelled Tertian Fever. It refers to a fever where the symptoms are felt every third day (or, in practice, every *other* day—the 'third' being the "day after tomorrow." It's what we call malaria, mosquito-borne fever.

Berecynthia the beldome of the Gods

Berecynthia is not a misprint, but rather an obscure goddess name. Berecynthia is an epithet of Cybele that is related to Mount Berecynthus, named after a priest of Cybele, Berecynthus. **"Beldome"** as printed is unknown. It's not in the OED. I'm certain the author intended ***beldame***, which is in the OED, meaning venerated grandmother or great-grandmother. Shakespeare uses "beldame" in *Lucrece*:

To shew the beldame daughters of her daughter... [Lucrece 953]

The English Secretary 1586 does have a short "faults escaped" section but beldome was missed. In fact, the editor asks the readers to correct all remaining mistakes as they are found: "The residue the learned reader may correct with discretion."

ferendum est quod mutari non possit

This is obscure, but is real Latin. In context I suggest it means something like "What cannot be done, change brings about."

Saint Margerie

"St. Margerie," a unique expression, might refer to **Saint Margaret the Virgin,** the most popular in England of many Saint Margarets, with over 250 churches dedicated to her.

However, if **Saint Margaret of Scotland** is implied, there are some interesting connections: She was the granddaughter of Edmund Ironside. Her father was Edward Atheling, Saxon heir to the throne, but exiled in Hungary where Margaret grew up. Her brother was Edgar Atheling, dubbed the "Earl of Oxford" by King Harold *before* the first de Vere Earl of Oxford. Margaret's husband, prince Malcolm, had been just a child when his father, King Duncan, was killed by Macbeth. In 1054 Macbeth was driven out—Malcolm became King of Scotland and Margaret become Queen. Malcolm was killed in a battle with English forces in 1093. Three days following, Margaret died. And there's another factor. Edward de Vere's mother was Margerie Golding; her name appears again in *The English Secretary,* as a woman, not the saint.

Non nobis solum nati sumus

This was easier to identify; it's from Cicero's *De Oficiis,* 1.22, meaning "We are not born for ourselves alone." Cicero says he translated the phrase from Plato's Letter to Archytas. The meaning is one of comradeship and citizenship. We have a civic duty to feel kinship and behave in a friendly and kind manner.

thou canst not choose

This phrase is particularly interesting. In the letter above and the examples that follow the meaning is not an "inability to choose among several things." It means compelled by circumstance. No choice. In Oxford's letters we have:

> ...finding in them your request far differing from the desert of your labour, I could not choose but greatly doubt whether it were better for me to yield you your desire.

But more significant is the phrase's use in Shakespeare. In *The Tempest,* in Act I when Prospero has concluded telling Miranda his long story, and needs to meet Ariel in private, Prospero induces sleep in Miranda by the exact method developed hundreds of years later as the technique of hypnotic induction.

> Prospero Here cease more questions. Thou art inclined to sleep, 'tis a good dullness;
> And give it way. **I know thou canst not choose.** [Miranda sleeps]

In a commentary on this *English Secretary* letter to a widower, Jennifer Panek, in *Widows and Suitors in early Modern English Comedy* (Cambridge University Press, 2004) has some interesting remarks. Her book pays attention to situations such as in the above letter, where a husband inherits from a rich wife, married for that purpose. Panek says, regarding keeping the wealth by losing the wife:

> The celebration of precisely such an occasion is included, rather bizarrely, in Angel Day's *The English Secretary.* After a number of earnest examples of how to write a letter of condolence, Day offers, without comment, "An example consolatorie, pleasantly written to one, who has buried his olde wife," in which a bereaved husband is congratulated on his delivery from "a hateful and verie foule encombrance ... as wherewith you were continually cloyed by the nightly embracements of so unweildie a carcasse." **The letter continues in a jocular vein.**

Everyone has a keen eye for their own specialty but often miss the details lurking elsewhere. Thus, Panek thinks this letter is bizarre but the ones that precede it are "earnest." Actually, they are all bizarre.

As a final example for this section, I offer one of the "Epistles Amatorie" or "love letters" from the 1586 *English Secretary.* This one takes a highly unusual tone, if actual courtship were intended:

> **Mistress, what you are, I know not, and what I suppose you to be, I write not, only for that I find you in the place of a Gentlewoman, I determine for this season to entertaine you accordingly. And for that, my new acquaintaunce, is founded upon the deliverie of a disdainful message, take it not I pray you in scorn, that in some things I touch you, which have too far displayed your self by your needeless curiosity. Trust me, for mine own part, I neither looked to see you, much lesse to be offended for you. I understand you are nipped, I knowe not with what, and would be healed I know not by whom, for which cause, finding such niceness in your owne conceits, you are angry with Margerie, for keeping company with Marrian,** which moved you to utter such matter of modesty, that in advising an other to beware, you must affirme, that you could not chuse but laugh to see pleasure breed by liking, and trust upon trial. I am sorry beleive me, you past away with empty hands (being so well accustomed to lapfuls as you have been) & none in presence to greet you. I wish little soul your prettie else was an ace above 31 when you forgot your selfe so far, to utter more then your charge. For albeit you had in command to admonish, neither was it in your mistress' good pleasure, or pertinent to her courtesy, that you by scoffing objections should scorn others, in things especially whereunto in truth they were never parties, and the cause not concerning your self, whom to be plain with I do suppose to have as litle discretion in the same, as you had consideration in delivery of the rest. **For which cause wishing you in his behalf, whome I love, to refraine your privy skoffs without occasion, and envy without desert, who for the Vertues in him appearing deserves more allowance, then at the hands of a better then your self might very well have perceived, I herewith end my letters.**

The beginning is a masterpiece of put down. **"Mistress, what you are, I know not, and what I suppose you to be, I write not, only for that I find you in the place of a Gentlewoman, I determine for this season to entertaine you accordingly."**
If you are missing the sense of it, let me translate: "Honey, I don't know what you are or what you think you are. I wouldn't write except that you are 'in the place of' a gentlewoman—so I will entertain you as such."

Scorn—Oxford uses "scorn."

> ...my Lord, leave that course, for I mean not to be your ward nor your child, I serve Her Majesty, and I am that I am, and by alliance near to your Lordship, but free, and **scorn** to be offered that injury, to think I am so weak of government as to be ruled by servants, or not able to govern myself.—To William Cecil, Lord Burghley

> I beseech your Majesty in whose service I have faithefully imployed my self, (I will not intreate that you suffer it youre self thus to be abused) but that you will not suffer me thus to be flouted, **scorned** & mocked.—To Queen Elizabeth

> In constant troth to bide so firm and sure,
> To scorn the world regarding but thy friend,
> With patient mind each passion to endure,
> In one desire to settle to thy end?—from "Love Thy Choice"

"I knowe not with what". In Oxford's letters we have:

> "...the quantite, is but frivolous, and **I know not to what** purpose..."... And **I know not by what** better means, or when her Majesty may have an easier opportunity ...

> … it appertains to have heard my cause, but **I know not why or with what** advice it was referred to Master Attorney and his Majesty's Counsel in Law…

"for which cause". In Oxford's letters we have:

> The Masters of the Mine Tins are constrained to keep a multitude at work upon the Mines, for which cause they are forced and have used to borrow money of the Merchants before hand.

Margerie—perhaps it's a coincidence, but Margerie was Oxford's mother's name.

could not chuse—as above, this time matching exactly the example from Oxford's letters. Oxford also uses the spelling, chuse, on occasion.

CHAPTER FOUR

A black hole inside conventional scholarship on Angel Day

SEVERAL PIECES are missing in most conventional scholarship on Angel Day and his books:

- A whitewash of Oxford's name and relationship to Angel Day in both old and new Dictionary of National Biography (the DNB).
- A related dereliction, by numerous top scholars, who have written lengthy papers on The English Secretary without ever naming the Earl of Oxford.
- A mystification extending to others in Oxford's circle, such as Thomas Bedingfield.
- An inability of current scholars to review and assimilate previously published biographical information about Day.

First, it will be useful to offer, in full, the old DNB entry for Day and the new DNB entry as well.

Old Dictionary of National Biography:

DAY, ANGELL (*fl.* 1586), miscellaneous writer, was the son of Thomas Day of London, parish clerk, and was bound apprentice to Thomas Duxsell, citizen and stationer in London, for twelve years from Christmas day 1563, He published in 1586 a curious and entertaining manual of epistolary correspondence, entitled *The English Secretorie wherein is contayned a perfect method for the inditing of all manner of*

Epistles and familiar letteres. Black letter, 4to; reprinted in 1587, 1592, 1599, 1607, n.d. [1610?], 1614. His other works are: a pastoral romance entitled *Daphnis and Chloe. Excellently discribing the weight of affection, the simplicitie of love, the purpose of honest meaning, the resolution of men, and disposition of Fate, &c.,* 1587 black letter, 4to; a poem in six-line stanzas, *Upon the life and death of the most worthy and thrice renowned Knight,* Sir Philip Sidney, &c., 4to, 6 leaves; and *Wonderful Strange Sightes seene in the Element, over the citie of London and other places,* n.d. (circ. 1585), 8vo. Some commendatory verses by Day are prefixed to Jones's *Nennio,* 1595.

Comments on the above:

- The old DNB has no mention of Day's named patron, the Earl of Oxford.

- The old DNB was mistaken about the existence of an 1587 edition. There is no extant version from that year and the 1592/93 edition doesn't mention any intervening editions. Rather, the 1592/93 refers in its epistle specifically back to the first edition of 1586. **The actual dates of publication are 1586, 1592/93, 1595, 1599, 1607, 1614, 1621, 1625, and 1635.** The book remained in print for five decades, with up to 7,000 copies or so in total circulation. **Every edition of *The English Secretary* featured a dedication to Oxford at the front.**

- The DNB was incorrect about Angel Day and the Wonderful Strange Sightes pamphlet. That little book names its author inside, Thomas Day, and dates the miraculous sky event at 1583. More on this below.

New Dictionary of National Biography:

Day, Angell (*fl.* 1563–1595), stationer and writer, was the son of Thomas Day (Daye), parish clerk. Though little is known of his personal life, Day was apprenticed to Thomas Duxsell, stationer in London, in 1563, beginning his service on Christmas day of that year. By 1575 Day probably had completed his apprenticeship; however, he next distinguished himself as the compiler of a handbook for epistle writing entitled *The English Secretorie,* printed first in 1586 in London by Robert Waldegrave and sold by Richard Jones. Day's book was so successful that it was reprinted in 1592 and again in 1595, 1599, 1607, and 1614. Other subsequent printings occurred: one identified as 'now newly revised', which Pollard and Redgrave dated at 1618, and later printings which are identified as having been printed in 1621, 1625, 1626, and 1635. There also appears to have been a printing of the second part of the book alone in 1614. By the time of its final printing *The English Secretorie* had been in print regularly for almost fifty years.

The second printing of the book, entered in the Stationers' register in 1587, but not printed finally until 1592, was dedicated to Sir William Hatton, to whom Day had appealed for patronage in his dedication to Daphnis and Chloe, also published in 1587.

Encouraged perhaps by the success of this early work, and urged on by the popularity of pastorals such as Edmund Spenser's *Shepheardes Calendar* (1579), Day produced an adaptation of *Daphnis and Chloe*, a pastoral romance translated from the Greek into French by Jacques Amyot (printed in 1559). Day's version appeared in 1587 (also printed by Robert Waldegrave). Since its republication in a facsimile edition (1890, ed. Joseph Jacobs) literary critics have noted the poem's overt nationalism, with its idealized depiction of Queen Elizabeth as a symbol of England. Today Day's translation of *Daphnis and Chloe* survives in only one copy, now housed in the collection of the British Library.

Day's other literary work was more modest in scope and stature. In 1595 he published commendatory verses, *Nennio, or, A Treatise of Nobility,* a translation of the Italian humanist treatise by William Jones, 'gentleman', printed by Peter Short, who produced the 1599 edition of *The English Secretorie.* Two additional pieces are frequently attributed to Day. The first is the printing of a poem in six-line stanzas entitled *Upon the Life and Death of the most Worthy and Thrice Renowned Knight, Sir Phillip Sidney* by Robert Waldegrave in 1587 bearing the authorial initials 'A.D.'. The second is a pamphlet (not dated, but thought to be c.1585) entitled *Wonderfull Strange Sightes Seene in the Element, over the Citie of London and other Places.*

Nothing is known of Day's life beyond the details of his apprenticeship and his publications. Although biographers have assumed that he gave up a career as a stationer in order to pursue his writing there is, in fact, no evidence to corroborate this. If nothing else, Day's consistent association with printers such as Robert Waldegrave and booksellers such as Cuthbert Burbie and Richard Jones suggests that he retained close ties with the world of printers and booksellers throughout his literary life.

S. P. Cerasano, 'Day, Angell (*fl.* 1563–1595)', *Oxford DNB*, Oxford University Press, 2004

Comments on the above:

Once again, there is no mention of Day's patron, the Earl of Oxford. Instead, author Cerasano commits a devious piece of faux-scholarship/disinformation. Note that he writes,

> The second printing of the book, entered in the Stationers' register in 1587, but not printed finally until 1592, was dedicated to Sir William Hatton, to whom Day had appealed for patronage in his dedication to *Daphnis and Chloe,* also published in 1587.

This is extraordinarily misleading. The 1592 edition (actually, January 1593 by our calendar), was dedicated right up front to the 17th Earl of Oxford (as before, in 1586) and bears, again, Oxford's coat of arms, with his motto, Vero Nihil Verius, as had the first edition in 1586. What is different is that ***in a single copy,*** held at the Folger (one of the few extant copies of the 1592/93 *Secretary*), ***there is a second dedication*** at the head of the new Tropes section of the book.

Cerasano's first indirection in the new DNB is that he only mentions one "patron" in association with Angel Day— the semi-obscure Sir William Hatton. This finely-parsed bit of data is presumably offered to pre-empt any intelligent reader's unasked question, "precisely for whom did master-secretary Day work?"

The second piece of selective truth telling is that the Folger-owned 1592/93 copy's second dedication section is actually made to three men together, gentlemen who all fall within the circle of the Earl of Oxford: Francis Gawdy, Sir William Hatton, and Thomas Bedingfield. They are linked to Oxford by documentary, historic facts. This triple-dedication is, therefore, something extremely interesting and useful. For the complete discussion of this matter go to Chapters 17-21, pages 49-56.

Cerasano repeats the old DNB's statement about Angel Day and the *Wonderful Strange Sightes* pamphlet. Anyone who takes the trouble to look at the book, which is of a religious bent, neither humorous nor instructive, will see that the author's name, Thomas Day, is given inside, and his style is unlike anything associated with Angel Day. Pollard and Redgrave's *Short Title Catalog* properly assigns the book to Thomas Day. One must conclude that the present DNB contributor didn't even bother to check. Moreover, we know from the apprentice log at Stationers' Hall that Angel Day's father was Thomas Day, parish clerk. A church bookkeeper. Could not the father be the author of the *Wonderful Strange Sightes* pamphlet so frequently misattributed to his son?

CHAPTER FIVE

Who was Angel Day?

BEFORE WE GO ANY FURTHER, we must ask, "who was Angel Day?" While a full biography of Angel Day would be impossible, he was, indeed, a real person and some important, basic facts are known.

We first learn of Day from the Stationers' Register. An extant entry shows that on December 25, 1563, he was bound as an apprentice stationer to one Thomas Duxsell, a freeman of the company. The entry reads:

> Thomas Duxsell : Angel Daye, the sonne of Thomas Daye of London, paryshe clerke, hath put hym self apprentice to Thomas Duxsell, Citizen and Stacioner of London from the feaste of the byrth of our Lorde god 1563 Twelve years &c ....
> vj (d)

Duxsell, as did his fellows, had to pay sixpence [the notation vj (d)] to register his apprentice. Angel Day's actual birth date remains undiscovered. However, the custom in London at that time was for an apprenticeship of a *minimum* of seven years, but with the consideration that the optimum age for release from apprenticeship— becoming a freeman of the company—was at the age of twenty-four. [Plant, Marjorie, *The English Book Trade,* London, 1939, pp. 131-139.]

A typical apprenticeship began around age 16 or 17, so, by that rule of thumb, it is possible Day was born circa 1546-47. However, the *12-year* apprenticeship of Angel Day suggests he may have been around the age of 13 when entered as an apprentice in 1563, which would give him a birth year of 1550, the same year Edward de Vere was born. Oddly, this is precisely the date Renaissance scholar Robert O. Evans (see below) guess-timates for Angel Day, 1550. Even giving a few years in either direction as margins of error, Angel Day was of the same generation as Edward de Vere, both born under the brief reign of Edward VI, who was child-King from 1547 to 1553.

While the above apprenticeship is as far as most modern scholars have gone with Day's personal biography, there is actually more data out there, simply forgotten or missed by 99 percent of modern commentators. If you read a dozen academic papers on a highly specialized topic you will quickly notice that the authors all quote from and refer to each other's articles. If there is new factual information on an obscure topic, it is immediately absorbed by the reigning experts in the field. Unless they have all missed it, because the data is outside of their normal sources, or someone in the chain disliked the data and suppressed it.

In this case, I think the Day experts simply missed the fact that there were several discoveries about Angel Day posted in *Notes and Queries* in the 20th century that bear very much on understanding Day, his occupation, and relations.

New Facts #1 from Notes and Queries

In the August 13, 1938, edition of *Notes and Queries*, Jean Robertson contributed a short article on Angel Day, whom she was researching for *The Art of Letter Writing*, 1942.

She found in the records of the proceedings of the Court of Requests for the year 1584 (Bundle 51/6 – held in the Public Records Office) a bill and answer of three disputants, one Hugh Machlyn versus Angel Day and William Tracy. Robertson's study of the matter led to her conclusion that this named Angel Day was the Angel Day of *The English Secretary.*

Machlyn's Bill of Complaint reads, in part,

> That whereas one Anne Moore did dwell and was servant with Angell Daye of London, Skryvenor, and whereas also by a confederacy betwene the said Angell Daye a very shifting fellow & of bold life, and one William Tracye, two very bold and lewd persons intending to cosen and decieve your said subject it was imparted to him by the said William Tracy what a great marriage the said Anne Moore was.

Whether Machlyn's assessment of Day and Tracy was biased or not (it was) certain facts emerge that do bear out as truth.

1. Day lived in London in 1584.
2. He was a professional scrivener.
3. He apparently lived in his own household, and for a short time, at least, employed a servant, Anne Moore.
4. Day was married (not to Anne Moore). [see below]

Robertson's further analysis includes:

Anne Moore was the daughter of one Edward Moore of Shropshire who had apparently left her the lease of an estate that earned £40 a year. Machyln was considering a marriage with Ms. Moore and was interested in her legacy. In Day's testimony he says that he had spent £40 traveling to Shropshire and back investigating her claim's veracity. Machlyn then paid Day £17 in cash, £3 worth of butter and cheese, and entered into a bond of £20 to pay Day a further £17 and another bond of £20 to pay Tracy £13. Machlyn then married Anne Moore, fully expecting to capitalize on her inheritance, only to discover that the lease and the entire deal were, in his eyes, counterfeit.

Day's response is dated July 2, 1584, and headlined, "The joint and several answers of Angel Daye Gent and William Tracy defendantes to the slanderous and untrue bill of complainte of Hugh Machlyn, complainent."

Here is the next excerpt Robertson published in N&Q, which may have been penned by Day, but just as likely by his lawyer: (spelling modernized)

> … the said Anne at her first coming to London which was about Easter now last past a twelve month was brought unto the house of the said Angel Daye by a brother of hers, named Edward Moore, to be his servant, but the said Angell Daye and his wife finding her altogether unfit for that purpose after two or three days or thereabouts as this defendant now remembreth put her away. And after a few days that she had been absent she returned againe to the house of this defendant and to his wife made pitiful lamentation and moan beseeching her for God's cause to take her again for that else she knew not whether to go … whereupon moved with compassion she [Day's wife] tooke her in and was content to lodge her for a season until otherwise she could provide herself.

Robertson continues explaining that Anne told Day about the lease and he believed her. In a detail oddly reminiscent of the most modern Internet e-mail scams, Anne told Day that a mere £3 repayment (to a certain widow who held the paper) would release the valuable lease to Anne. Day offered up the £3, retrieved the lease and (allegedly) traveled all the way to Shropshire (a major journey even today!) to check out the truth of the claim. However, Day hightailed back to London when he heard by letter that Anne Moore was selling the same lease to others in his absence! He threw her out of the house and demanded that she raise the funds elsewhere to pay him back. At that point she moved in with William Tracy where she met one Rowland Hodgeson, who brought his friend Hugh Machlyn over to interest Hugh in marrying Anne.

The conclusion of the defense claims that it is the complainants who are the shifty ones in this case:

> … without that these defendants were ever noted or informed to be shifting fellows or men of loose life or conversation or did ever seek to become motioners or makers of any marriage … by blazing the said Anne to be a great marriage … the said defendants have ever remained in their several vocations of good men, fame and reputation, without ever being touched in any such vile and base practices and the accusation that the said complainant is so slippery a fellow that by his own companions it hath bene reported to these defendants that (not caring for his wife) he meaneth to make what money he can by the said lease and to go no man knoweth whether.

In other words, Day and Tracy are upstanding men and blameless, while Machlyn is simply unhappy with his wife and has made up this whole business, causing the defendants to lose time and money.

As always, the truth must be somewhere in between. Perhaps this historical tidbit is ignored because it might throw Mr. Day into a bad light.

I agree with Robertson. What are the chances that there would be a second professional scribe (scrivener) named Angel Day in London at exactly the same time as Angel Day the secretary? She checked, and there are no other persons of the time in London named Angel Day in *any* profession.

This new information humanizes Day; he was self-employed at that time, working for various clients; he had enough income to support a wife and household, risk small investments, and travel at great time and distance on the slim chance of gain. On that last point, I don't believe that Day went to Shropshire, let alone twice, as claimed in his defense, in pursuit of such a dubious profit. Could he be so naïve? Nevertheless, something happened; bonds were encumbered, money changed hands, and dissatisfied parties took the case to court. Sadly, Robertson does not report a verdict in the case. Perhaps the matter was thrown out for being ludicrous. These facts are true: In 1584 Day had a house in London with his wife and was a professional scribe.

New Facts #2 from *Notes and Queries*

As is often the case in *Notes and Queries,* one published "new fact" leads to another contributor sharing a related new fact. In the November 12, 1938, edition of N&Q, a follow-up disclosure about Angel Day was contributed by none other than Warren B. Austin, of The College of the City of New York. Warren B. Austin later on became a pioneer of literary stylometrics when he published, in 1969, the results of his two-year U.S. government-funded computer study of Greene's *Groatsworth of Witte* and concluded that the author was Henry Chettle. Austin is something of an expert on Chettle and Gabriel Harvey and the others in the "University War of Wits."

Austin, back in 1938, apparently intrigued by Jean Robertson's find that Angel Day was married and had a household, made a search for the correspondent marriage entry in the published volumes available in the United States. He found it in the Parish Register of Christ Church, Newgate Street, which reads:

> **1582 [1581] December 4, Angell Daye (of Lyons Inne) & Frauncis Warley, by license.**

Austin explains:

1) A systemic error of unnecessary correction was imposed on these registers when they were published by the Harleian Society.
2) Frances Warley was possibly the daughter of Thomas Warley (servant to Mr. Clark, a butcher). T. Warley's death on Nov. 25, 1581, is noted in the same register and Austin says that it was rather typical to see a daughter marry immediately after the death of a father, perhaps due to a sudden cessation of a father's opposition to a marriage.
3) Austin says, "At any rate, Day is now provided with the wife referred to in the Court of Requests action of 1584. His connection with an Inn of Court, moreover, would automatically entitle him to the designation, 'Angel Daye, Gent.,' we find he used in his answer to the bill against him.

I agree with Austin's conclusions and would correct him only on one point: that Lyons Inne was, in fact, an Inn of Chancery, and not an Inn of Court (law school).

Lyons Inne

Located among the Inns of Court near the Inner Temple stood Lyons Inne. Lyons was not an Inn of Court but an Inn of Chancery. The Inns of Chancery were preparatory schools for the Inns of Court to which they were attached. Chancery students learned about documents, writs, subpoenas, mastered secretary and chancery handwriting, forms of address, basic legal affairs, how to draw up legal papers of all sorts, etc. But without additional training in the Inns of Court, they could not argue cases at the bar; they did not practice law; they were "Gents" and not "Esquires." Many Chancery interns went on to become clerks, government functionaries, or secretaries to aristocrats.

Lyons Inn

By the 15th century there were four Inns of Court that granted law degrees, the Middle Temple, the Inner Temple, Gray's Inn, and Lincoln's Inn. In addition there were ten Inns of Chancery, each one a subordinate or "feeder" institution for one of the Inns of Court. Thus Lyons Inn, Clifford's Inn and Clement's Inn were all associated with the Inner Temple. By the mid-16th century there were only eight Inns of Chancery. The most recent loss was in 1549 when Protector Somerset requisitioned Strand Inn from Middle Temple, and they never got it the property back.

In 1561 Middle Temple tried to wrest control of Lyon's Inne, but

their efforts were thwarted by a special effort by Robert Dudley, Earl of Leicester, who was a dedicated life member of Inner Temple, and the Queen. As a result, Leicester was rewarded with a gala celebration at the Inner Temple's Christmas Revels of 1561. There, Dudley became head of a new "Order of the Pegasus" and, after 1561, Pegasus, the winged horse, became the emblem and arms of the Inner Temple. Interludes for the 1561 Revels were drafted by Arthur Broke, the young, doomed, credited author of *Romeus and Juliet,* the juvenile poem that is a significant source for *Romeo & Juliet,* and saw the first performance of *Gorboduc,* by two Inner Temple men.

Members of the Inner Temple figure prominently in this study. Many of its members, the elite of London's barristers, serjeants-at-law, and their honorees, play roles more than incidental to the "Shakespeare" affair.

Inner Temple men included: **Robert Allot** (*England's Parnassus 1600* – with Oxford poems), **Francis Beaumont** (playwright), **Arthur Broke** (*Romeus and Juliet*), **Sir Thomas Bromley, Sir Julius Caesar, Robert Devereux, 2nd Earl of Essex, Sir Edward Dyer, Robert Dudley, Earl of Leicester, Sir Francis Gawdy, Arthur Golding** (*Ovid's Metamorphoses,* Oxford's uncle), **Sir Christopher Hatton, Philip Herbert Earl of Montgomery** (Oxford's step-son, named co-sponsor of the First Folio), **Henry Howard** (Oxford's enemy), **Roger Manners, John Manningham, Thomas Norton** (*Gorboduc*), **Sir Thomas Sackville Lord Buckhurst** (*Gorboduc*), **Anthony and Thomas Sherley, Thomas Skinner,** (another Oxford adversary), **Henry de Vere 18th Earl of Oxford** (admitted April 20, 1605), **William Underhill** (see Chapter 21), **Thomas Wentworth** (Ashbourne portrait owner). Broke, Golding, P. Herbert, and Henry de Vere were "specially admitted," i.e., they were not trained barristers.

Shakespeare (the author) mentions Inns of Court and Chancery only a few times.

Prince — Go bear this letter to Lord John of Lancaster, to my brother John; this to my Lord of Westmoreland.

Go, Poins, to horse, to horse; for thou and I have thirty miles to ride yet ere dinner time.

Jack, meet me to-morrow in the Temple Hall at two o'clock in the afternoon; there shalt thou know thy charge. *[1Henry IV, III.2]*

SCENE 4 – London. The Temple garden

Enter the EARLS OF SOMERSET, SUFFOLK, and WARWICK; RICHARD PLANTAGENET, VERNON, and another LAWYER

Plantagenet Great lords and gentlemen, what means this silence? Dare no man answer in a case of truth?

Suffolk **Within the Temple Hall we were too loud;** The garden here is more convenient.

[1HenryIV, Act III Scene 3]

In 2Henry IV we have Shallow remembering his days at Clement's Inn, also linked to the Inner Temple:

Shallow A must, then, to the Inns o' Court shortly. I was once of Clement's Inn; where I think they will talk of mad Shallow yet.

Silence You were call'd 'lusty Shallow' then, cousin.

[2Henry IV, Act III Sc 2]

There are three more mentions of Clement's Inn by Shallow in the same play; but nowhere else in Shakespeare.

Shakespeare also mentions Gray's Inn:

Silence This Sir John, cousin, that comes hither anon about soldiers?

Shallow The same Sir John, the very same. I see him break Scoggin's head at the court gate, when 'a was a crack not thus high; and the very same day did I fight with one Sampson Stockfish, a fruiterer, behind Gray's Inn. Jesu, Jesu, the mad days that I have spent! and to see how many of my old acquaintance are dead!

Silence We shall all follow, cousin.

[2Henry IV Act III. Scene 2]

Gray's Inn formed the nexus of an entirely separate clique, an equally powerful club of legal men centered, in Elizabethan times, around Lord Burghley. Gray's Inn was the law school of Edward de Vere, 17th Earl of Oxford. For our purposes, these are the significant **Elizabethan-era Gray's Inn members:**

Francis Bacon (lawyer, essayist). **Robert Bertie, first Earl of Lindsey** (1582–1642, eldest son of Peregrine Bertie, 13th Baron Willoughby and Mary, daughter of John de Vere, 16th Earl of Oxford; Bertie was Edward de Vere's nephew). **Thomas Campion** (1567-1620; Gray's Inn revels of 1588; songs for the *Gesta Grayorum* revels, 1594). **Robert Cecil, 1st Earl of Salisbury** (Oxford's brother-in-law, correspondent, and adversary). **William Cecil Lord Burghley** (Lord Treasurer, Oxford's step-father). **John Chamberlain** (1553–1628, letter writer who mentioned 1,000 Londoners by name, but never

"Shakespeare"). **John Clapham** (1566–1619, writer-editor; career service to Lord Burghley; Clerk to the Lord Treasurer ~1590; wrote *Narcissus* 1591). **Francis Davison** (writer-compiler: *A Poetical Rhapsody* 1602—has anonymous and "A.W." poems variously argued for Shakespeare or for Oxford, *Anagrammata* 1603—has tribute to Edward de Vere; Francis was the son of William Davison who carried the death warrant for Mary Queen of Scots). **Robert Dewhurst** (son of Oxford's associate, Bernard Dewhurst, who was an estate manager and surveyor in the employ of Lord Burghley. **Abraham Fraunce** (poet-lawyer; *Lamentations of Amyntas* for the death of Phillis). **George Gascoigne** (poet-soldier; associated with Oxford through *100th Sundry Flowres*). **Everard Guilpin** (satirist; *Skialetheia, or, A Shadowe of Truth* 1598). **Edward Hall** (*Hall's Chronicle,* a key source used for Shakespeare's history plays). **Sir John Hayward** (historian-lawyer; wrote *1st & 2nd parts of the life and raigne of King Henrie IIII;* was interrogated in Essex investigations). **Sir Thomas Heneage** (both Vice Chamberlain and Treasurer of the Chamber in the 1590s, husband of Mary Countess Southampton). **Sir Charles Howard Baron Effingham Lord Admiral** (friend of Oxford and theatrical patron of Admiral's Men). **Thomas Howard 4th Duke of Norfolk. Francis Kinwelmersh** (poet, collaborator with Gascoigne, verses with Oxford's in *Paradyse of Daintie Devices*). **John Lyly** (writer; secretary to 17th Earl of Oxford, special admittance to Gray's Inn, 1594 for the Revels). **Francis Norris Earl of Berkshire** (1579–1622; Oxford's son-in-law; married Bridget de Vere). **Thomas Powell** (writer: *A Welch Bayte to Spare Provender* 1603 ded. to Henry Wriothesley, Southampton), **Robert Rich 1st Earl of Warwick** (~1559–1619; married Penelope Devereux, Essex's sister who was adored by Sidney, probably as "Stella"). **Sir Philip Sidney** (poetic and personal rival to Oxford). **Ferdinando Stanley, Lord Strange, 5th Earl of Derby** (patron of Strange's Men, Derby's Men, playing some anonymous dramas now called Shakespeare's). **William Stanley, 6th Earl of Derby** (Oxford's son-in-law; married Elizabeth de Vere). John Twyne (father of Thomas Twyne, a doctor who dedicated *Breviary of Britain* to Oxford, and Lawrence Twyne, who wrote *Pattern of Painefull Adventures,* a source for *Pericles*). **Edward de Vere 17th Earl of Oxford. Sir Francis Walsingham** (originator of Her Majesty's Secret Service). **Henry Wriothesley third Earl of Southampton** (1573–1624; bailed out of arranged marriage to Oxford's daughter; dedicatee of *Venus & Adonis* and *Lucrece,* friend of Henry de Vere 18th Earl of Oxford)`. **Richard Barnfield** was not a member but wrote dedications to Gray's

Inn men in *The Encomion of Lady Pecunia,* 1598). The Hales v. Petit law case featured in *Hamlet* was a Gray's Inn case; Justice Sir James Hales was a Gray's Man. (See Anderson, pages 34-35)

Gray's Inn had its own theatrical traditions. Gascoigne's *Supposes* and *Jocasta* debuted there in 1566-1567. The *Gesta Grayorum* revels of 1594 featured "a comedy of errors" that is widely thought to be the first performance of the play attributed to Shakespeare.

While key information on Angel Day has been public since 1938, none of the academic writers on Day and his work have assimilated these central new facts: his association with Lyons Inne, his profession as scrivener, his court case, and his marriage. This paper is the first to draw all biographical sources together for Angel Day.

Additional short biographies of Day were published in the *Dictionary of Literary Biography* in 1996 and 2001.

Richard Rambuss in *Sixteenth Century Non Dramatic Writers, Third Series* [DLB vol. 167, 1996] repeats and condenses what he wrote for *English Literary History 59* (1992), reviewed below. Rambuss, in the DLB, never mentions Oxford, and, while naming just about every other major writer of the English Renaissance, he manages to never mention Shakespeare either. It appears that the anxiety about Day's relationship with Oxford is matched by nervousness about Day's influence on Shakespeare. Better to leave all that stuff out. Yet he leaves breadcrumbs of doubt and confusion as he wanders through this dangerous thicket. Rambuss writes,

> In *The English Secretary* Day implies that at some time he served as a secretary himself (and thus is writing from personal experience); he does not mention however, whose secretary he was. Since no further biographical records exist, the shape of Day's career is best gleaned from his publications.

Rambuss could have spent more time looking at the publications rather than extrapolating on what his predecessors had written. When we consider the 1586 dedication to Oxford and its revisions in 1592/93, 1595, and 1599, the thirteen year span, the statements in the dedications themselves, and the continuation of the place of honor in his book strongly argue that Oxford was the lord for whom Day practiced his secretarial skills, which included utmost discretion and the keeping of the master's secrets.

Judith Rice Henderson of the University of Saskatchewan penned the first real biographical improvement for Day in 2001's *Dictionary of Literary Biography Volume 236, British Rhetoricians and Logicians*

1500-1660. Henderson, though unaware of the facts uncovered by Robertson and Austin that were published in *Notes and Queries,* 1938, still does a better job with the material at her disposal than the previous biographers did. Henderson writes at the outset,

> Jonathan Goldberg and Richard Rambuss have observed Day's emphasis on the obligation of the Elizabethan secretary to secrecy in conducting the affairs of his employer. Yet scholars have not shown enough interest in Day's life to penetrate its mysteries. **Clues in his works suggest that he used his rhetorical skills not only to instruct others in the duties of a secretary but also to serve the Elizabethan regime.**

Henderson uses the corrected dating and recognizes that *English Secretary* edition #2 came out in early 1593 by our calendar. I was gratified to read that Henderson (alone among the mainstream scholars) is in agreement with me that Angel Day did ***not*** write *Wonderful Strange Sightes seen in the element* ... She tracked down this attribution error to W. Carew Hazlitt in his *Handbook to the Popular, Poetical and Dramatic Literature of Great Britain,* 1867. Apparently Hazlitt didn't bother to look inside where the book is clearly credited to Thomas Daye. All scholars until Henderson, and the present writer, accepted Hazlitt at face value, and obviously never bothered to look at the pamphlet in question. I did, and I share Henderson's conclusion that the most likely author is Thomas Daye, parish clerk, Angel Day's father. Henderson also reasons, reasonably, I think, that the sort of fanatical Protestant who would name his son "Angel Day" (i.e., the day of the Apocalypse, "Judgment Day," etc.), could be just the sort of person who, on seeing bright lights in the sky on September 2, 1583, (likely a rare low-latitude display of the *aurora borealis*) immediately wrote a pamphlet saying he had seen a sign of the impending Judgment Day. Because the printer, Robert Waldegrave, would go on to print *The English Secretary* 1586, and Day's *Daphnis and Chloe,* 1587, added to Day's own experience and connections as an apprentice Stationer, it is not unreasonable to conjecture that he arranged the printing of his father's pamphlet.

Henderson, who takes all of Day's statements at face value, has trouble therefore reconciling the slender autobiographical hints he provides into a coherent chronology. Angel Day is maddeningly circumspect and opaque in his self-references and shows an overall reticence to self-revelation. In my view of a thinly veiled dual authorship of *The English Secretary,* Day's enigmatic statements make more sense, though I doubt many (if any) orthodox scholars will follow me down the rabbit hole on that conjecture. Day, in 1586, and 1592/93 offers a convoluted and barely credible history of his book, its revisions, and troublesome publication birth pangs. It's a shaggy dog story, and offered, I suggest, to befuddle and misdirect readers away from thinking about how the book actually came to be. For example, in the 1592/93 main revision the preface writer says the book's revised edition was delayed by the demands of his "present profession" and the book-seller's desire to sell out the first edition in full before reprinting. Day says specifically that in the intervening time period between editions [1586-1593], he had little time because "...my profession will not suffer it being otherwise occupied in my place and calling and that very diversely." In short, Day is saying that the professional demands on his time as a secretary disallowed the time needed to attend to his book. Yet the revised edition was registered in 1587; other factors delayed the book's printing by five or six years. Then, Henderson jumps to an unfortunate wrong conclusion. She assumes that the dedication to Gawdy, Hatton and Bedingfield in front of Part II in 1592/93 means that Day had been secretary in those intervening years to Gawdy. She ignores the fact that the dedication to Oxford is still at the front and that Day has entirely rewritten the dedication to reflect the time that has gone by. The one thing that hasn't changed from 1586 is Day's continued avowed service to Oxford. In fact, Day makes it clear in his letter to Gawdy, Hatton, and Bedingfield that he is thanking them in advance **"without any merit of my service",** that is, he has never worked for them. Reading carefully he says he has met only Bedingfield. What Gawdy, Hatton, and Bedingfield had in common was that that they all knew the Earl of Oxford, not that they all knew Day.

Henderson thinks Day wrote all the example letters except for the very interesting example in the 1586 edition alone, which purports to be a letter from the Elizabethan diplomat, Robert Bowes, to Henry Carey, Lord Hunsdon. [This letter can be read here in Chapter 25.] I don't think it is an authentic letter of Bowes. It is identical in style to the rest of Day's example letters, and a large number of Bowes' actual letters have been published, and the "Bowes letter" in the 1586 *English Secretary* is not that of the careful diplomat to Scotland. In any case the letter was removed (along with several others) from all subsequent editions. Henderson draws attention to several examples (that did carry over to editions following) that she finds inherently amusing, the epistle to "Egregious doctors" (in the category of what not to say), the recommendation of a worthless servant, and the consolation to a bereaved wife. I agree. These three could all serve as the foundations for classic British comedy.

Henderson mentions that the Skelton letter and surrounding explanation were also removed from following editions. She appears unaware of the scandalous nature of the censored verse, the double-action Folger copy, and the article about Day's contribution to Skeltoneana. [See Chapter 24]

Henderson also notices the peculiarities in the original love-letter section that is unique to the 1586 edition. She posits that the love story in the 1586 *English Secretary*'s "Epistles Amatorie" (where suitor "B.L." courts "Mistress Mawdlin") was a direct imitation of the love story in *The Image of Idleness* 1555, often called the first English novel told in the form of letters. In that book the contrasting correspondents are called "Walter Wedlocke" and "Bawdin Bachelor." The *idle* title may have served to inspire the name *The Enemie of Idleness,* by Fulwood, 1581, which was a much more sober approach to letterwriting (described below) and the very book Day was about to dethrone with his own manual. Henderson acknowledges that Day dumped the colorful 1586 "love letters" for a rather dry set of examples on proper pre-marital epistolatory intercourse. She quotes Baldwin, who found the 1592/93 replacement letters, **"impeccably correct, arid, academic, and uninteresting."**

Henderson correctly notes that starting with the 1592/93 revision, Day weeds out details, specific links to real events and persons, and this culling continues with the 1595 and 1599 editions. Henderson is also perceptive enough to see some of Day's authentic dilemmas. She writes,

> Day struggled with certain issues. If the secretary is not the equal of his master in social status, how can he be a friend? ... How far should self-denial go? Day wrote in admiration of an Irish boy who died trying to protect his English master, Captain Henry Davells, from assassination by the rebel Sir John of Desmond, but he considered this sacrifice a child's irrationality, for it did not save Davells. On the other hand, a servant to the Turkish ruler, who had assisted the Christian traitor Scanderbeg out of fear, at last made the honorable choice to die for his fault rather than wade farther into treason. Day did not face all issues quite so squarely. He offered in 1593 (but in 1599 omitted) a story of a secretary who successfully dissuaded his master from treason. What if the master had not been dissuaded? Day derived the word *secretary* from *secret*, but should all confidences be kept? When is it appropriate to lie for the sake of loyalty?

She brings up some interesting points for our study. First, is the out-of-the-blue example of the story of George Scanderbeg, which occupies several pages, to teach the moral of the honest and loyal servant/secretary. From other sources we know that Oxford was interested in

Scanderbeg. [For more on Scanderbeg, see Chapter 22.]

Captain Henry Davells was real. He was assigned, along with many others, to put down the Second Desmond Rebellion in Ireland in 1579, and he was indeed assassinated by John of Desmond (John Fitzgerald).

The treason story is fascinating. Day concocts the example of a noble citizen of **Mantua** named Roderigo, who plans a conspiracy against the Duke, but is dissuaded by his loyal secretary. The only Shakespeare play with a Roderigo is *Othello* where he is an unwitting part of Iago's conspiracy. Roderigo kills Cassio, is killed by Iago, but **letters** in his pocket reveal Iago's plot. Mantua figures in the plot of *Two Gentlemen of Verona* and in *Romeo & Juliet* when Romeo goes into exile in Mantua. Virgil was from Mantua. In two articles in the *Shakespeare Oxford Newsletter* 2003, "Ten Restless Ghosts of Mantua," John Hamill noted important connections between Shakespeare, Mantua, and Oxford. These links include the mention of Gulio Romano in *Winter's Tale,* the mural of the Rape of Lucrece seen at the Ducal palace, the presence of Aretino and Castiglione in Mantua, the Gonzaga connection to *Hamlet*, and more. In any case, *The English Secretary*'s nod to Mantua fits in a larger pattern of interest. [Henderson's comments on *Daphnis and Chloe* are addressed in Chapter 8.] Henderson is also the first of the mainstream commentators on Angel Day who figured out that Thomas Beddingfield Esquire equals Thomas Bedingfield, Esquire, translator of *Cardanus Comfort,* and associate of the Earl of Oxford.

Next, Henderson finally acknowledges the presence of the Earl of Oxford in Day's life and this book. She is one of the first (in several hundred years of short Day biographies) to break that barrier. Of course, she tries to minimize Oxford's role by saying that Day's dedications were, in general, to "courtiers of the Queen," such as Oxford, Walsingham, and Sir William Hatton. Henderson gets it right when she admits:

> In 1593, Day acknowledges Oxford's 'so great bounty' when he presented the first edition to him 'five years passed,' and the earl may have continued to reward subsequent editions of *The English Secretary* for the dedication to him is changed slightly through each edition up to 1599.

This is true, and as Oxford is the only dedicatee to get this kind of continued special treatment, why resist the idea that Day provided secretarial service to Oxford? We know he employed secretaries throughout his career, and also that the epoch of John Lyly as Oxford's secretary and Anthony Munday as Oxford's secretary was ending just as Angel Day emerged on the scene.

The only other modern writer to acknowledge that the 17th Earl of Oxford was in Day's circle of acquaintance is **Lynne Magnusson,** in ***Shakespeare and Social Dialogue: Dramatic language and Elizabethan Letters,*** Cambridge University Press, 1999. Magnusson "broke the ice" two years before Henderson. She writes,

> Angel Day's letter-writing handbook has this double agenda. On the one hand, Day presents an interactional rhetoric inscribing social discriminations in subtler ways than the highly status-conscious handbooks of the medieval *ars dictaminis.* By promoting this rhetoric that reinforces the place of the superior, even in the invisible grain of the language, Day might hope to please noblemen like the Earl of Oxford, to whom he dedicates his book. For his less exalted readers, Day offers the skills requisite to write and speak like the Earl of Oxford and lesser gentlemen, or—perhaps more important—the skills to write *to* or speak *with* those of importance."
>
> Clearly Angel Day sees *The English Secretary* as "a tool for 'making places' in the social order"—not only for his readers but also for *himself.* ... He recommends himself as well as his book to the Earl of Oxford, emphasizing the "will I have to do unto your Lordship *any acceptable service.*"
>
> Day elevates and mystifies the competence required of a secretary, putting it outside the reach of most readers, at the same time as he displays (despite the modest disclaimer) his own capacity to take on this important office.

Later, without any sense or irony or inter-relation, Magnusson compares Day's style of studied social correctness with the skills employed in the two dedication letters from "Shakespeare" to Henry Wriothesley in *Venus and Adonis* 1593 and *Rape of Lucrece* 1594.

Beyond this, Magnusson is mostly interested in displaying her own mastery of rhetoric, as in the semiotic academic jargon of literary deconstruction, such as: "Day's extended treatment of request-making exemplifies this more subtle figuring of social relation. As with Erasmus, Day's epistolary rhetoric resembles Brown and Levinson's politeness theory in its classification of letter types into speech-act categories."

CHAPTER SIX

The English Secretary in Renaissance studies, communication studies, and the history of letter writing

THE ENGLISH SECRETARY holds a special place in the history of communications. Prior to 1586, the following books were available in English that touched on general utilitarian rhetoric and letter writing and were generally available in the later 16th century.

Richard Taverner, ***The garden of Wysdom 1539;*** Thomas Wilson, ***The Arte of Rhetoric 1553;*** revised in 1560; Richard Rainolde, ***The Foundacions of Rhetorike 1563;*** William Fullwood, ***The Enimie of Idlenesse, 1568*** [Fulwood's manual teaches letter writing by formula, featuring translations of foreign authors and based on the French *Le stile et maniere de composer, dicter, et escrire toute sorte d'epistres, ou lettres missives...;* Abraham Flemming, ***A Panoplie of Epistles, Or, a looking Glasse for the vnlearned 1576,*** contains letters translated from 57 famous authors, including Aristotle, Ascham, Brutus, Cicero, Erasmus, Macropedius, Plato, Socrates, Zeno; and Henry Peacham, ***The Garden of Eloquence 1577.***

Books in foreign languages that were very influential included: Erasmus' ***De conscribendis epistolis 1521;*** Vives' ***De conscribendis epistolis 1537;*** Georgius Macropedius' ***Methodus de conscribendis epistolis 1580.***

Despite the fact that few modern persons (other than Oxfordians) have even heard of *The English Secretary,* there is an abundance of scholarship on Day's secretarial manual, in the histories of business, communications, and core influences on Elizabethan and Jacobean authors.

Robert O. Evans, now a professor emeritus in English at the University of Kentucky published a re-issue of the 1599 version of *The*

English Secretary in 1966. His comments are fascinating for what they say and what they do not say. Evans claims that the DNB "dismisses summarily" *The English Secretary* by providing this parsed snippet of their description, a *"manual of epistolary correspondence."* Actually the old DNB gave this sentence:

> He published in 1586 a **curious and entertaining** manual of epistolary correspondence, entitled *The English Secretary, wherein is contained a perfect method for the inditing of all manner of Epistles and familiar letters ...*

It's Evans who is being dismissive. And, as the DNB, in both old and new versions, saw to it to erase the name of Edward de Vere in connection with Angel Day's biography, so also does Evans manage to never mention the name of de Vere, even though he reproduces, photographically, Angel Day's 1599 dedication to the Earl of Oxford. Evans discusses the fact that secretaries of that era were normally attached to the household of a noble man, if not the royal court. He mentions the theory that Spenser may have been, as a young man, secretary to the Earl of Leicester. Why was Evans too nervous about Oxford to even mention him? Perhaps because at the end of his introduction he gently brandishes his own pet theory: that William Shakespeare worked with Day's manual on his desk!

> ... no one can say whether or not books like Day's ever found their way into the ordinary grammar schools of the sixteenth century, such as the one Shakespeare must have attended.
>
> Books like *The English Secretary* surely found their places on many a writing table. It is debatable whether Shakespeare could have named, or even described with any accuracy, the vast variety of figures, or even a portion of them, that appear in is plays. But that he employed them deliberately in a conscious artistic manner is almost beyond the bounds of argument, certainly it is for scholars whose attention has recently been directed to rhetoric.
>
> It can be ascertained that Shakespeare, for one, learned his lessons well. An examination of Day's figures will quickly reveal that, while he speaks of them as ornaments, they are sufficiently comprehensive to include, as Sister Miriam Joseph says, almost all the realm of rhetoric. But Shakespeare does more than use the figures as ornamentation to beautify his works. As I have suggested (in *The Osier Cage, an essay on the Rhetoric of Rome and Juliet*), he employed the figures functionally to emphasize the development of plot and character. It seems to me likely that he did not rely entirely on his memory of his grammar school training for the information he needed. There is at least a strong likelihood that he kept some manual beside him, and as Day's is in certain respects the best and most popular it may very well have been the book he used. More than that we cannot at present speculate.

Another article by Richard Rambuss, from 1992, is remarkably instructive, showing the extent to which one can see some profound truths about Angel Day, without comprehending his precise cultural setting. The paper is: "The Secretary's Study: The Secret designs of *The Shepheardes Calender*," Richard Rambuss, *English Literary History* 59 (1992) pp 313-335. Rambuss first uses the example of "EK," the glossary-maker and "editor" of Spenser's *Shepheardes Calender*, to demonstrate, quite literally, how Elizabethan secretaries kept secrets, how studies were done in a study, and how "privy matters" were private affairs. While the yet-unknown EK served faux-secretarial functions for Spenser, the poet Spenser himself was serving as the actual secretary to John Young, Bishop of Rochester. Rambuss writes,

> The link between secretaryship and secrecy was regularly asserted in the period, but perhaps never more saliently than by Angel Day, who insists repeatedly in his letterwriting manual *The English Secretary* that a secretary is foremost "a keeper or conserver of the secret unto him comitted." Day substantiates this claim by uncovering *secret* at the root of the word *secretary*, so that "by the verie etimologie of the worde it selfe, both Name and Office in one, doe conclude uppon secrecie." Day thus fashions a secretary who literally *is* his office, *is* the privy place where his master withdraws to store secrets. Just as "we do call the most secrete place in the house, appropriate unto our owne private studies...a Closet," he notes, "the partie serving in such place may be called a Secretorie...as hee is a keeper and conserver of secrets."

Rambuss also has this to say about Day's book:

> Angel Day's *English Secretary* was not only among the most popular letterwriters of its time, it was also the most ambitious. To begin with, Day's was the first English letterwriter declaring itself to be **comprised almost entirely of original letters.**

Previous "letterwriter" books/manuals in English offered only translated examples from classical and humanist writers. While Rambuss assumes that Day composed the sample letters himself, Day's testimony itself is more ambiguous. From the 1586 edition: "Almost all of which Epistles before set downe were nowe sodenly by the Author ordered and invented to their severall examples."

That's a marvelously equivocal statement. The "Author" is capitalized; would it not be conceited and vain to say that about yourself? Perhaps another Author invented the letters and put them "in order" to fit Day's scheme. Or, perhaps, Day is the conceited Author, but he has "ordered" them (as one would order dinner) and they were invented to serve as Day's several examples. Or one can read it on the surface, conceited Day is proud that he has invented and put in order these fanciful letters. In any case they are admitted to be "inventions."

Rambuss goes on to present his theory that the relationship between a Master and his Secretary was so close and intimate that a "Closet" relationship may be reasonably inferred in many cases. And he *does* mean what you think he means. Rambuss writes,

> It is the secretary's duty, Day continues, to observe his master's habits so that he can be "a zealous imitator in all thinges, to the intent that *knowing the effects of his Lord, with what ends and purposes they are varied, and unto what forms and manner of writing he is speciallie addicted*" (2:130). **As imitator in all things, one of the things the secretary must imitate is the master's hand, even to the extent of being able to replicate his signature — the sign(ing) we have come to recognize as the authenticating discursive mark of individual subjectivity.** Concurrently, the secretary should also know how to read his master's mind, being able to anticipate his "ends and purposes". Day's agenda thus goes beyond the notion that the secretary's skills need to be commensurate with the status of the man he serves. More than this, Day articulates the process by which a secretary comes to don his master's self. Secretaryship does not simply mean transcribing, copying down the words of the master; it entails **becoming the simulacrum of the master himself.** That is how the secretary is, in Day's word, "accomplished" (2:13). It is a commonplace of Renaissance discussions of secretaryship to make the management of secrets the primary business of this office. We have already noted the private and markedly affective terms Cecil uses to describe what is transacted between the master and the secretary: their "counsels" are like "the mutual lections of two lovers," which necessarily remain secret, "undiscovered to their friends."
>
> Once a secretary has found out such "hidden secrets," he must be careful to lock them away, advises Robert Beale, Clerk to the Privy Council, within "a speciall Cabinett, whereof he is himselfe to keepe the Keye, for his signetts, Ciphers and secrett intelligences." The figure of the locked and hidden cabinet (or its synonym in these discussions, the closet) recurs throughout Faunt's and Day's treatises as well, but Day goes further by troping on this trope and making the secretary himself the closet in which the master's secrets are stored. The closet is the place for the "reposement of secrets," "the most secret place in the house," Day reminds us, and then concludes that "in respect of the covertnes, safetie and assurance in him . . . the partie serving in such a place may be called a Secretorie." **Day carries the correlation between this servant and his office** to point of metaphorizing the secretary's body as ideally itself a closet. "To a closet," he notes, "there belongeth properlie a doore, a locke, and a key" (2:103). Similarly, since the secretary is in Day's phrase **"but the closet, whereof another hath both the key, use and commandment,"** he ought to be "as a thick plated doore, where no man may enter, but by the locke which is the tongue, and that to be of such efficacie, as whereof **no counterfeite key should bee able to make a breache"** (2:124). The secretary is his office.

I am reminded of Prospero's complaint against his scheming brother in *The Tempest.* He says, "... *having both the key of officer and office,* set all hearts in the state to what tune pleased his ear." Rambuss concludes,

> Day goes on to describe this closet—and, metonymically, the secretary himself—as the place "where our dealings of importance are shut up, a roome proper and peculiar to our selves" (2:103). It is the place for writing, the place "appropriate unto our owne private studies," for which "we keepe the key our selves, and the use thereof alone doe onelie appropriate unto our selves." This secret room—and this secretive servant—is, in Day's striking formulation, the space in which we "doe solitairie and alone shut up our selves." One cannot help noticing Day's repeated invocation of the language of the self here, as well as his registration of a formative relation between writing, secrecy, and subjectivity: in the secretary's closet (among other places in early modern culture) an interior, private subjectivity begins to be scripted and secured. Here the self is coming to be formed in and as its secrets. Fittingly, secretaries were called "inward men" in the Renaissance. **And no wonder Day's secretary—a closet in which is closed up his master's secrets, his master's (secret) self—is able to simulate his master, to be both his servant and his imitator "in all thinges."**

I find these remarks fascinating, especially as Rambuss is apparently unaware that Day had just this relation with Oxford, and their work is arguably the work of two men whose purpose was one, in exactly the manner imagined by Rambuss. In his notes, Rambuss points out that in the first edition of *The English Secretary,* 1586, Day clearly acknowledges his indebtedness to Erasmus and other rhetoricians for both the structure and theory of his book. However, **this acknowledgement was omitted from all subsequent editions.** Rambuss attributes this to what he imagines is Day's vanity and aspirations towards higher regard by contemporaries and history. The actual reasons may be more complex.

CHAPTER SEVEN

Day and Shakespeare— unpleasant correspondences

IN SURVEYING the academic literature—with an eye out for scholars who have innocently recorded connections between the words of Day and Shakespeare—pearls can be found. But, like Robert O. Evans, discussed above, they present their briefs briefly, and exit stage left before anyone asks any questions. Examples follow.

J. L. Simmons, writing in *Shakespeare Quarterly* (27.3, Summer 1976), presents "Holland's Pliny and *Troilus and Cressida.*" Simmons hones in on Pandarus' bold question in *Troilus and Cressida,*

> "Is this the generation of love? Hot blood, hot thoughts, and hot deeds, why they are Vipers, is Love a generation of vipers?" [*Troilus and Cressida,* III, I, 126-8]

He duly notes that this is a send-up on a biblical phrase, "O generation of vipers, who hathe warned you to flee from the wrath to come?" [Matthew 3:7 and other similar lines elsewhere] But Simmons argues Shakespeare was influenced more immediately by Philemon Holland's translation of Pliny's *Natural History,* 1601. While many readers might take Pandarus' words in a modern sense, i.e., 'Is this the love generation? Is this a generation of vipers?' that's not what is meant at all. Think of generation as the act of generation, the act of pro-creation. According to Pliny (and the Elizabethans, of course, believed him), Viper snakes generate in a violent manner with the mother often getting eaten as a reward for passion. Now we get to the point of this digression. Simmons notes that an earlier example of the exact phrase is found in *The English Secretary* (1592/93 and forward).

> Between a Trope and a Scheme the difference is, that the Trope changeth the significations, as in these words Generation of Vipers, meaning thereby homicides of their own issue or ancestors, as the Viper devoureth her own brood.

Michael Cameron Andrews' article, "His mother's Closet: A note on *Hamlet*" appeared in *Modern Philology* November 1982. His focus is the moment in *Hamlet,* Act III, scene 4, when Hamlet meets his mother in her "*closet.*" Andrews argues that most modern commentators have applied Freudian thinking to this scene by insisting (in criticism or theatrical direction) that the fateful meeting takes place in the Queen's bedroom. This allows many layers of psychosexual Oedipal speculation. But Andrews correctly shows what Shakespeare wrote. The closet appears three times in the play. First in association with Ophelia, second and third with Gertrude.

Pol. How now, Ophelia? What's the matter?
Oph. O my lord, my lord, I have been so affrighted!
Pol. With what, i' th' name of God?
Oph. My lord, as I was sewing in my closet,
Lord Hamlet, with his doublet all unbrac'd,
No hat upon his head, his stockings foul'd,
Ungart'red, and down-gyved to his ankle;
Pale as his shirt, his knees knocking each other,
And with a look so piteous in purport
As if he had been loosed out of hell
To speak of horrors- he comes before me.
Pol. Mad for thy love?
Oph. My lord, I do not know, But truly I do fear it. [Hamlet 2,1,75~]

The second instance:

Ham. Make you a wholesome answer; my wit's diseas'd. But, sir, such answer is I can make, you shall command; or rather, as you say, my mother. Therefore no more, but to the matter! My mother, you say—
Ros. Then thus she says: your behaviour hath struck her into amazement and admiration.
Ham. O wonderful son, that can so stonish a mother! But is there no sequel at the heels of this mother's admiration? Impart.
Ros. **She desires to speak with you in her closet ere you go to bed.**
Ham. We shall obey, were she ten times our mother. Have you any further trade with us? [Hamlet 3,2,310~]

Scene IV. The Queen's closet. *Enter Queen and Polonius.*

Pol. He will come straight. Look you lay home to him.
Tell him his pranks have been too broad to bear with,
And that your Grace hath screen'd and stood between
Much heat and him. I'll silence me even here.
Pray you be round with him.

Ham. *(within)* Mother, mother, mother!
Queen. I'll warrant you; fear me not. Withdraw; I hear him coming. [Polonius hides behind the arras.]

Andrews then points out the meaning of closet in other Shakespeare plays and its contemporary meaning in general. It was not a bedroom, but a private room where one could have a conversation. A private sitting room as we would call it. Andrews notes that the OED gives only one late-Renaissance example of "closet" as a private room prior to *Hamlet* 1603/04. It's Day's *English Secretary:*

> ... we do call the most secrete place in the house, appropriate unto our owne private studies and wherein we repose and deliberate by deep consideration of all weighty affairs, a Closet, in true intendment a place where our dealings of importance are shut up ...

The OED is actually incorrect about the date. The quote appears in the 1592/93 and subsequent editions of *English Secretary,* not 1586 as claimed. The oft-noticed King James Bible (1611) reference ("... the bride out of her closet," Joel 2:16) is too late to have influenced *Hamlet.*

Patricia Parker contributed an article, "Othello and Hamlet," In the book, *Shakespeare Reread: The texts in New Contexts*, (Ross McDonald, ed.), in which she discusses distrustful advisors, servants, and ministers of state. Parker writes,

> The link between "secrets" and "secretories" is everywhere emphasized in the world contemporary with *Hamlet*, in contexts that overlap with secrecy in the realm of espionage and spies. The "secretorie," as Angell Day puts it in *The English Secretorie,* is the keeper of "secrets and counsels," a trust that linked the office of Principal Secretary with the monarch's "closet" or "secret Cabinet."

Parker warns that a lord with a secretary had to be very careful because of the possibility of betrayal. Parker restates Day's premise as, "The secretary is the closet of his lord and place where this master deposits secrets." Parker and others note that a closet relationship is a close relationship, especially in privy matters, and go on to suggest the similarity of these secret relationships to what we would term as homosexuality.

Parker makes a more interesting point where she highlights Day's statement that for a faithful secretary "his pen in this action is not his own." The secretary according to Day must subjugate his personality and faithfully become the voice of his master. Then Parker compares this to Hamlet's situation where he feels he is a mere secretary to the ghost of his father, using words faithfully recounted (instead of manly deeds) to enact a revenge and complains, "...that I, the son of a dear father murthered, prompted to my revenge by heaven and hell, *must like a whore unpack my words,* and fall acursing like a very drab." *[Hamlet 2/2/582-6]*

CHAPTER EIGHT

Daphnis and Chloe

DAY IS RESPONSIBLE for the first translation into English of the antique Greek romance, *Daphnis and Chloe,* 1587. Day translated not from Greek but from the popular French edition of Jacques Amyot. The book's long Euphuistic title reads:

> Daphnis and Chloe Excellently describing the weight of affection, the simplicitie of love, the purport of honest meaning, the resolution of men, and disposition of Fate, finished in a Pastorall, and interlaced with the praises of a most peerlesse Princesse, wonderfull in Maiestie, and rare in perfection, celebrated within the same Pastorall, and therefore termed by the name of The Shepheards Holidaie. By Angell Daye. Altior fortuna virtus. At London printed by Robert Waldegrave & are to be sold at his shop in Paules church-yard at the signe of the Crane 1587.

The charming plot of *Daphnis and Chloe* tells the story of long-ago Arcadia; of two abandoned baby foundlings, a boy, Daphnis (found with a sword), and a girl, Chloe (found with golden accessories), who were both adopted by rustic families. As teenagers the two became innocent friends; an event that involved Daphnis falling into a pit allowed another suitor, Dorco, to pursue Chloe, but without success. The two continued their young courtship with many acts of playful flirtation. Daphnis' name is associated with the sacred tree of Apollo, the laurel, which first emerged from the nymph Daphne.

Chloe's name evokes the bright green of springtime. As in chlorophyll, the name is related to the Greek *khloros,* meaning, the color "bright yellow-green." In the middle of this verdant idyllic pastoral, Tyrian pirates emerge from over the horizon and carry away Daphnis and steal Dorco's oxen. But Chloe, armed with the dying Dorco's panpipe,

Daphnis and Chloe

EXCELLENTLY
deſcribing the vveight
of affection, the ſimplicitie of loue, the purport
of honeſt meaning, the reſolution of men, and diſpoſi-
tion of Fate, finiſhed in a Paſtorall, and interlaced with the praiſes
of a moſt peerleſſe Princeſſe, wonderfull in Maieſtie,
and rare in perfection, celebrated within
the ſame Paſtorall, and therefore
termed by the name of

The Shepheards Holidaie.

By ANGELL DAYE.

Altior fortuna virtus.

AT LONDON
Printed by Robert Walde-graue, & are
to be ſold at his ſhop in Paules church-yard
at the ſigne of the Crane.

1587.

Daphnis and Chloe title page.

plays the oxen-come-home song, and they leap off the ship, capsizing the vessel. Daphnis hurries home by acting as yoke to two swimming oxen. They bury Dorco and attend to the wine harvest.

When an old man, Philetas, tells an elaborate tale of love, Daphnis and Chloe realize for the first time that *they* are "in love." They try to acquire *remedies* against it, as if love were a terrible affliction. Next, Daphnis endures another abduction attempt, this time by the cruel and near-unpronounceable Methymnaeans. When the Methymnaeans returned they managed to carry off Chloe. Daphnis prays to Pan and is promised a positive outcome. In a scene that is an unacknowledged influence on *The Tempest,* Pan, (like Ariel at Prospero's command), creates a monstrous faux-storm of imagination and terrifies the captain into releasing Chloe and the stolen goats and sheep. Next there is much celebration and retelling of the myths of Pan and the nymphs. Daphnis and Chloe have more adventures together and exchange vows. Next spring, Daphnis learns a lesson in love from an older woman, but remains virginal with Chloe. He offers to tell Chloe the story of Echo in exchange for ten kisses. He tells the tale and she gives a thousand kisses. Daphnis has not been considered by Chloe's foster-father, Dryas, who senses she is of noble birth and is holding out for a better match than another shepherd like Daphnis. But Daphnis has a vision of the location of a hidden treasure. He goes and uncovers it and offers the loot as a wooing gift to Dryas. Before the wedding can occur, many mishaps and new vile suitors appear (in gimmicks still used by Hollywood) to slow the inevitable. Finally, through a series of fortuitous circumstances, the two lovers' birth-tokens are revealed, families reunited, and the marriage of two bluebloods, Daphnis and Chloe, finally occurs.

Along the way there is much erotic allusion in the Greek original, though parts of the story were lost to the Renaissance translators and readers, and Amyot held back much titillating detail. Day redacted even more, reflecting the respective levels of prudishness in their societies at the time of publication.

At one point in the history of Shakespeare scholarship, *Daphnis and Chloe* was proposed (and accepted in many quarters) as an additional source of *The Winter's Tale.* This attribution has gone out of fashion. In the recent and otherwise excellent *Shakespeare's Books,* by Stuart Gillespie, 2001, Mr. Gillespie is dismissive: "Wolff, 1912, offers a now generally discounted suggestion about Day's *Daphnis and Chloe* as a source for *The Winter's Tale.*" I suppose "generally discounted" is not as bad as "generally discredited."

The Arden edition of *The Winter's Tale,* edited by J.H.P. Pafford in 1962, was a bit more evenhanded:

> There is also slight evidence that Shakespeare may have made some direct use of Angel Day's version of *Daphnis and Chloe* 1587, which is one of the sources of *Pandosto*. ... The straying of sheep hardly needs rationalization but even here Shakespeare adds a reason. Wolff notes that Shakespeare could have taken details directly from Angel Day's version of *Daphnis and Chloe* (1587) or have borrowed them from *Pandosto.* But one detail, that of the hunt, is in Day but not in *Pandosto.*

The relevant quote from Wolff is given below. Day's 1587 *Daphnis and Chloe* directly influenced Robert Greene's *Pandosto,* 1588. It is *Pandosto* that always takes the credit now as Shakespeare's principal influence or source for the plot of *The Winter's Tale.* But Wolff showed that in several instances, Shakespeare was reading Day's version and not just Greene's because of certain added details that Shakespeare carried over from Day, and not from Greene or Amyot.

The most significant is acknowledged when Wolff describes a passage in Day's *Daphnis and Chloe* that was used to great effect by Shakespeare:

> ... a passage which gives him both means to punish Antigonus and the means to drive the sheep to the seaside. This is the incident of the young Methymnaeans' hunting, the noise of which frightens the sheep and goats from their upland pastures down to the shore. What more consonant with dramatic economy that that Shakespeare should have borrowed this hunt, and have used it both to send the bear that devours Antigonus, and at the same time to frighten the sheep away from the hills so that the shepherd must seek them along the shore and there find the child. This, at any rate, is the use Shakespeare has made of the hunt. Now the motif of the hunt is not in Greene; there is no reason to suppose that Shakespeare invented it when it lay ready in his hand in Day's version of *Daphnis and Chloe.*

Henderson noticed (without any apparent sense of wonder) how Day inserted into the *Daphnis and Chloe* narrative a number of poems and songs. Henderson catalogs the many meters and styles employed: "...poulter's measure (iambic couplets with the first line in hexameter and the second in heptameter), fourteeners (fourteen syllables arranged in iambs), and quatrains (four line stanzas). Strangely, we have examples of Oxford using just these archaic meters. [See Steven W. May, *Elizabethan Courtier Poets*]

Amyot's version (first edition in 1559), tells the story in three parts. Day has removed the framing device and all of section three to make room for his own inclusion (that has nothing to do with the tale of Daphnis and Chloe) called *The Shepherds' Holiday.* Set on an imaginary island, the grand courtiers give tribute to their Queen Eliza.

Daphnis and Chloe features a character called *Meleboeus,* the Honey man. He is the main speaker. In most books he is spelled Meliboeus, after the speaker in Virgil's *Ecolog*.

Longus himself is a complete enigma. Nothing is known about him, as with Homer. The name may actually refer to the word Longus on one manuscript, which indicated it was the long version. *Daphnis and Chloe* may be a "generic" Greek-style adventure romance only ascribed to "Longus."

The story of Daphnis and Chloe takes place in Arcadia, the realm of Pan in ancient Greece. Though Sidney had reworked his *Arcadia* before his death in 1586, it was not printed until 1590 (incomplete) and 1593 (with revisions by his sister Mary), so Day's book *Daphnis and Chloe* preceded both Sidney's AND Spenser's book (*The Faerie Queene*) in telling a story of Arcadia in English.

Modern critical reaction to Day's version has not been kind. Yet it once again reveals the two-part nature of Day's work, one voice that is very fussy and prudish, and the other that is more euphuistic and hedonistic.

There is a lacuna (missing section) in the text. A key part of the story in the original Greek text was not available to Amyot in 1559 or for a Latin edition published in Florence in 1598. A manuscript of *Daphnis and Chloe* that had the section missing in the other copies was found in 1807 and published by PL Courier in 1809. What is remarkable is that Day seemed to know that there was a bit of narrative missing, even though he was working from the French translation. And Day filled in the missing details of plot, often accurately! Scholar Samuel Lee Wolff, in *The Greek Romances in Elizabethan Prose Fiction,* 1912, was the first to detail this, and considers Day to have made lucky guesses. It is never considered that Day or his sponsors might have had another source at hand, now lost.

Although Day cut most of Book Three from Amyot to make room for his political inclusion, the paean to Elizabeth, his *Daphnis and Chloe* sections are still longer than Amyot's. This is because of elaborate and unnecessary elaboration of the material. Wolff notes:

> Now where Longus and Amyot are simple, Day is composite. To Chloe's plain chaplet of pine he must add "all sortes of flowers." And when Chloe is likened to a nymph, he must liken her not only to a nymph but also to Leda and Io. ... When Amyot says that Daphnis saw Chloe, Day speaks of him as "fastening his earnest lookes on her admirable beauties ... wholie confused by Love the force whereof distilling amaine within him, had wrought to his most secret entrails."

But Wolff also complains that Day blurs the bright specific visual images of Longus and Amyot with vague dualities and unnecessary comparisons—writer's stuff. Richard F. Hardin's *Love in a Green Shade* (2000) looks at several thousand years of impact of *Daphnis and Chloe* on literature and culture. When he gets to Angel Day's version he concentrates on how much detail from Longus' story Day has cut out, specifically the most risqué or erotic scenes and conversations. Abandoning the Greek setting, Day's Arcadia is the English countryside of villages and noble manors.

Day deletes a bathing scene, the marriage sequence, and details of kissing. Hardin says, "Day often lets vividness dissolve into vagueness." He attributes all this to the requirements of Elizabethan society.

As noted before, Day ditched book three of the Greek *Daphnis and Chloe* to make room for his *Shepherd's Holidaie,* a fantasy of elaborate praise of Eliza. This book appeared in the same year as the execution of Mary Queen of Scots (February 8, 1587). The Armada was a only a year away. There was a great deal of nervousness in England and Day's puff piece was at once a salve, panegyric, and bid for royal favor. Meleboeus speaks of Mary's "deep deceipt" and promotes England's ascendancy in the New World.

Apparently, only one copy of Day's *Daphnis and Chloe* exists, and this led Joseph Jacobs (editor of *Daphnis and Chloe* in 1890) to postulate a suppression of the entire edition as not only copies are missing, but its impact was a soft glance. The printer of *Daphnis and Chloe,* 1587 was **Robert Waldegrave,** who became embroiled in the Marprelate scandal in the same year. Henderson postulates that when Waldegrave's shop was raided on April 16, 1588, that all copies of *Daphnis and Chloe* were seized along with his Marprelate stock. There is no proof of this, but it is possible. The issue becomes infinitely more complicated when we add to the equation the fact that Justice Francis Gawdy was one of the principal government investigators of the Marprelate publications.

Henderson speculates that Angel Day was employed to spy on Robert Waldegrave and that he was chosen because of his already forged link to Waldegrave, and his connection to Gawdy. Day had dedicated his Sidney epitaph to Francis Walsingham (Sidney's father in law, who practically bankrupted himself staging Sidney's incredibly expensive funeral). Walsingham was, at that time, England's spymaster. So, while Henderson's theory is plausible, it remains unproven; there are aspects to Day's career that she has not taken into due consideration.

Wolff criticizes Day for emphasizing "ridiculous and even

contemptible aspects of rustic manners and character that altogether omits irony …" Isn't it interesting that "Shakespeare," who is traditionally tied to a rustic life lived mostly in a rural, farming area, still found a way to belittle the little people in the plays, rather than praise or ennoble their behavior? Was this "nose-up to the downtrodden" a trait also shared by Angel Day? Was Day really another uppity social climber with an oversized ego or did he simply serve as spokesperson for an aristocratic author?

Day deviates from his *Daphnis and Chloe* source by subtracting material wholesale to make room for his own embellishments. However, in addition to these story changes, **Day's publication of Daphnis and Chloe adds eight unique lyrical songs interspersed into the action of the Greek adventure tale.** They are songs, sonnets, and poems. Some of these are rather good, and are better than other verses ascribed to Day. [See Chapter 27 for the text of these songs and poems.]

CHAPTER NINE

The English Secretary as a bestseller

WE HAVE SEEN how important *The English Secretary* was in its time. Before we examine the book's structure in greater detail, let's first examine the book's bibliographical history. It was a bestseller and stayed in print for some fifty years.

A Bibliographic History of The English Secretary

Copyright:

Stationers' Register November 7, 1586

Richard Jones - Receaved of Richard Jones for pryntinge The Englishe Secretarye. By warrant under master Warden Byshops hand and the booke Compiled by ANGELL DAYE ....vjd

Also Robert Walgrave by his handwryting did consent to this entrance in Richard Jones his name.

This requires some comment. Richard Jones established copyright of *The English Secretary* in his own name with the consent of Robert Waldegrave, who actually printed the book. Richard Jones' long career in London (imprints from 1565-1602) was more often as a named bookseller than as printer, but he did print many books. The most interesting curiosity of this entry is: "the booke Compiled by Angell Daye." The word "compiled" is not typical. "Compiled" does not appear on the 1586 title page. It was not normal procedure to name an author in a Stationers' entry. It was neither forbidden nor encouraged. When a name is mentioned, there is often a strong correlation with a corresponding printed book that names the author on the title page. The 1586 title page (shown here facing page 1) puts ANGEL DAYE in capitals. It looks as if the entry clerk was looking at the quarto itself. Yet the odd choice of "compiled" suggests that either the clerk or Master Warden Bishop thought that Day had compiled the book, rather than written it, outright.

First Quarto, 1586:

The English Secretorie Wherin is contayned, A Perfect Method, for the inditing of all manner of Epistles and familiar Letters, together with their diuersities, enlarged by examples vnder their seuerall Tytles. In which is layd forth a Path-waye, so apt, plaine and easie, to any learners capacity, as the like wherof hath not at any time heretofore beene deliuered. Nowe first deuized, and newly published by Angel Daye. Altior fortuna Virtus. At London : Printed by Robert Walde-grave, and are to be solde by Richard Iones, dwelling at the signe of the Rose and the Crowne, neere vnto Holburn Bridge. 1586.

Dedication in the front of the book to Edward de Vere, 17th Earl of Oxford. Displays Oxford's coat of arms.

Secondary Copyright:

Stationers' Register January 10, 1586/87

Robert Walgrave – Receaved of him for printinge the second part of 'the Englishe secretarye ...vjd

Commentary: Just two months after *The English Secretary* was copyrighted, Waldegrave went to Stationers' Hall himself to copyright the second part, Day's treatise on Rhetoric and Tropes. By this entry we know that at least some significant portion of the new material slated for the revised *English Secretary* must have been ready by January 1586/87 for Waldegrave to invest sixpence in a book that was not ready to be reprinted. While *English Secretary* eventually sold well enough to go to nine editions, the momentum must have taken some time to develop. In only two months after *The English Secretary* first appeared enough copies had sold to convince Waldegrave of further investment. But not enough copies could have been sold from stock in the two months between Q1 and this second copyright to warrant printing a new edition. The owners (Jones and Waldegrave) would wait until all the Q1 stock was near depleted. However, Waldegrave never got the chance to see *his* profit. Caught up in the Marprelate scandal in 1588 his shop was raided and he left London, AWOL, and never returned. He printed overseas in La

Rochelle in 1589, and thereafter moved to Scotland, where he printed under an Edinburgh imprint from 1589-1603, when he died. When Waldegrave went into exile, Jones, who had a proven part interest in the book, now assumed the copyright entirely, probably with the Stationers' Company's approval. When a licensed Stationer had to flee, or was jailed, or died without a will, his copyrights would revert to the Company. As Jones was already involved in the book (and had the text copy) he was the first in line to assume the copyright. Thus the 1592/93 revised *English Secretary* bears only the name of Richard Jones.

Second Quarto, 1592/93, featuring extensive revisions and two new sections (see Figure overleaf):

> The English Secretorie, Or, plaine and direct Method, for the enditing of all manner of Epistles or Letters, as well Famillliar as others, destinguished by their diuersities vnder their seuerall titles. The like whereof hath neuer hitherto beene published. Studiouslie, now corrected, refined & amended, in far more apt & better sort then before, according to the authors true meaning, deliuered in his former edition : togeather (also) with the second part then left out, and long since promised to be performed. Also, a declaration of all such Tropes, Figures or Schemes, as either vsually, or for ornament sake, are in this Method required. Finally, the partes and Office of a Secretorie, in like maner, amplie discoursed. All which to the best and easiest direction that may be, for young learners and practizers, are now, newlie, wholelie and ioyntly published. By Angel Day. Imprinted at London by Richard Iones, dwelling at the Rose and Crowne neere Holborne Bridge. 1592.

Dedication in the front of the book to Edward de Vere, 17th Earl of Oxford. Displays Oxford's coat of arms.

Two copies of this book survive. In the Folger copy there is a second dedication in front of Part Two, a Declaration of Tropes, to Francis Gawdy, Sir William Hatton, and Thomas Bedingfield. This is the only instance of an additional dedication in all of the copies over 50 years.

Transer of Ownership:

Stationers' Register—June 25, 1595

> Cuthbert Burby—Assigned over unto him from Richard Jones by consent of the wardens and a Court holden this daye: A booke Intituled the English Secretary .... vjd.

This entry is important. First, the entry establishes that Jones indeed held full copyright after Waldegrave escaped, and now, with the full approval of the company, he was assigning copyright of *The English*

English Secretorie:

Or,

plaine and direct Method, *for the enditing*
of all manner of *Epiſtles* or *Letters*, aſwell *Familliar*
as others: deſtinguiſhed by their diuerſities vnder
their ſeuerall titles,

The like whereof hath neuer hitherto
beene publiſhed.

Studiouſlie, now corrected, refined & amended,
in far more apt & better ſort then before: according to
the Authors true meaning, deliuered in his former edition:
Togeather (alſo) with the ſecond part then left out, and long
ſince promiſed to be performed.

Alſo, a declaration of all ſuch Tropes, Figures *or* Schemes,
as either vſually, or for ornament ſake, are in this
Method *required.*

Finally, the partes and Office of a Secretorie, in like maner, amplie diſcourſed.

All which to the beſt and eaſieſt direction that may be, for young learners
and practizers: are now, newlie, wholelie and rightly publiſhed.

By Angel Day.

Imprinted at London by *Richard Iones*, dwelling at the
Roſe and *Crowne* neere Holborne Bridge.
1592.

The English Secretary, title page of the second quarto.

Secretary to Cuthbert Burby. The Stationers held a "Full Court Session" seasonally (at least four times a year) and additionally as required, when they would discuss matters of ownership along with other disputes and procedural matters. What probably happened was that a private Stationer-to-Stationer sale was arranged between Jones and Burby, and they simply had to wait for the next Full Court Session to establish their private arrangement with the Wardens of the Company. The sale to Cuthbert Burby (~1566–1607) is fascinating. His career, traced by imprints on his quartos, ranged from 1592–1607.

Cuthbert Burby was a publisher, a bookseller. He is never named as a printer. Among his earliest books, Burby was the named publisher of *Axiochus,* 1592, the strange book of translated pseudo-Plato (credited to "Edw. Spenser") that also contains the "Sweet Speech or Oration spoken at the Tryumphe at White-Hall before her Maiestie, by the page to the right noble Earle of Oxenforde." This oration describes the role of Oxford at a Tournament as "The Knight of the Tree of the Sunne." Burby published anonymous dramas in the 1590s such as *The Historie of Orlando Furioso* and *George a Greene the Pinner of Wakefield.* Burby published the anonymous *Taming of A Shrew,* 1594. Burby was the publisher of Nashe's *Unfortunate Traveler* in 1594 and *Lenten Stuffe* in 1599. Cuthbert Burby purchased *The English Secretary* in 1595 and immediately published the 1595 third edition, with an updated dedication to the Earl of Oxford. Burby published *Love's Labors Lost* 1598, often cited as the first Shakespearean play credited on the title page to "W. Shakespere." In a similar vein, Burby was the publisher in 1598 of *Palladis Tamia,* the book that names Oxford as "the best for comedy" while also introducing the authorial name, "Shakespeare," crediting him with plays as well as "sugred Sonnets among his private frinds." However, even though *Palladis Tamia* credited Shakespeare with the play *Romeo and Juliet,* when Burby published the book himself a year later, in 1599, *Romeo and Juliet* was published anonymously. Did Burby forget that "Shakespeare" was supposed to be the new brand name? In the same year that Burby re-established the anonymity of *Romeo and Juliet,* Burby again asserted his copyright on Day's manual and published the fourth edition and final revision of *The English Secretary* in 1599. Burby's version is the one that was copied through 1635, and the 1599 dedication to Oxford stayed with the book. Cuthbert Burby was an influential Stationer-publisher who was simultaneously connected to the 17th Earl of Oxford and to the name, "William Shakespeare."

Third Quarto, 1595, *minor revisions:*

The English secretorie: or, plaine and direct methode, for the enditing of all manner of epistles or letters, as well famillar, as others: distinguished by their diuersities vnder their seuerall titles, the like whereof hath neuer hetherto beene published. Studiously, now corrected, refined & amended, in far more apt & better sort then before: according to the authors true meaning, deliuered in his former edition: together (also) with the second part then left out, and long since promised to be performed. Also, a declaration of all such tropes, figures or schemes, as either vsually, or for ornament sake, are in this method required. Finally, the partes and office of a secretorie, in like maner amplie discoursed. All which, to the best and easiest direction that may be, for younger learners and practicters: and are now, newlie, wholelie and ioyntly published. By Angel Day. London: Printed for C. Burbie, and are to be sold at his shop, at the Royal Exchange. 1595.

Dedication in the front of the book to Edward de Vere, 17th Earl of Oxford. Displays Oxford's coat of arms.

Fourth Quarto, 1599, final revisions:

The English Secretary, or Methode of writing of Epistles and Letters, with A declaration of such Tropes, Figures and Schemes, as either vsually, or for ornament sake, are therin required. Also the partes and office of a Secretarie, devided into two bookes. Now newlie revised and in many parts corrected and ammended. By Angel Day. At London : Printed by P.S. for C. Burbie, and are to be sold at his shop at the Royal Exchange. 1599.

Dedication in the front of the book to Edward de Vere, 17th Earl of Oxford. No coat of arms.

Fifth Quarto, 1607, no revisions:

The English Secretary, or Methode of writing of Epistles and Letters with A declaration of such Tropes, Figures and Schemes, as either vsually, or for ornament sake, are therin required. Also the partes and office of a Secretarie, devided into two bookes. Now newlie revised and in many parts corrected and ammended. By Angel Day. London : Printed by T[homas] D[awson] for Cuthbert Burby, 1607.

Dedication in the front of the book to Edward de Vere, 17th Earl of Oxford. No coat of arms.

Sixth Quarto, 1614, no revisions:

The English Secretary, or Methode of writing of Epistles and Letters, with A declaration of such Tropes, Figures and Schemes, as either vsually, or for ornament sake, are therin required. Also the partes and office of a Secretarie, devided into two bookes. Now newlie revised and in many parts corrected and ammended. By Angel

Day. London : Printed by Felix Kyngston, for William Welby, and are to be sold at his shop in Pauls Church yard, at the signe of the Swan, 1614.

Dedication in the front of the book to Edward de Vere, 17th Earl of Oxford. No coat of arms.

Seventh Quarto, 1621, no revisions:

The English Secretary, or Methode of writing of Epistles and Letters, with A declaration of such Tropes, Figures and Schemes, as either vsually, or for ornament sake, are therin required. Also the partes and office of a Secretarie, devided into two bookes. Now newlie revised and in many parts corrected and ammended. By Angel Day. London : Printed by Thomas Snodham, 1621

Dedication in the front of the book to Edward de Vere, 17th Earl of Oxford. No coat of arms.

Eighth Quarto, 1625, no revisions:

The English secretorie, or, Methode of writing of epistles and letters with a declaration of such tropes, figures and schemes as either vsually, or for ornament-sake are therein required. Also the parts and office of a secretorie. Diuided into two bookes. Now newly reuised, and in many parts corrected and amended: by Angel Day. London : Printed by Thomas Snodham, 1625.

Dedication in the front of the book to Edward de Vere, 17th Earl of Oxford. No coat of arms.

Ninth Quarto, 1635, no revisions:

The English secretorie, or, Methode of writing of epistles and letters with a declaration of such tropes, figures and schemes as either vsually, or for ornament-sake are therein required. Also the parts and office of a secretorie. Diuided into two bookes. Now newly reuised, and in many parts corrected and amended: by Angel Day. London: Printed by W. Stansby 1635

Dedication in the front of the book to Edward de Vere, 17th Earl of Oxford. No coat of arms.

CHAPTER TEN

Differences between the first four editions

THERE ARE SIGNIFICANT differences in the first four editions of *The English Secretary*. These changes show the evolution of the book through successive revisions, eliminations, and additions.

First Edition - 1586

The Title page uses the spelling "Secretorie," which is used on the first three editions. The printer was Robert Waldegrave and the exclusive bookseller was Richard Jones.

This is the only edition of *The English Secretary* to use the motto, (though it also graces the title page of *Daphnis and Chloe* 1587): **Altior fortuna Virtus,** which means, "Virtue is higher than fortune."

The book begins with a long general section on letter writing and epistles that is trimmed to the bone in the later editions. The example letters consist of:

1 faux epistle
52 demonstration letters (five of which are cut out of all later editions)
7 "love letters" in a fictional frame—all eliminated in the later editions
60 total example letters in first edition

Second Edition – 1592/93

The Title page uses the spelling "Secretorie," which is used on the first three editions. The printer is stated to be Richard Jones, but the editors of the modern Short Title Catalog credit the printing to Thomas Orwin, and Jones was again the seller.

The second edition is entirely revised from the first. The author gives a long explanation of the revision process and blames the problems of the first edition on the demanding printers' schedules, misplaced manuscript pages, and severe time constraints. While Day seems to imply that the changes and new sections were made soon after the first edition, (and the copyright of "part 2" in 1587 supports this) there are other reasons to think the process took place in fits and starts over the six or so intervening years between the original and second quartos. While the conceit was that the second edition was perfected in all ways, the book is still riddled with errors, as was the first—everything from typos to mis-numbered pages. Also, some of the most unusual and interesting examples from the first edition were dropped. These failings, however, are more than made up for by the inclusion of the new material added to the book. A new section describes rhetorical devices or "figures" in great detail. New example letters were produced to illustrate this section. And Day added another section, of great interest, on the role and functions of a professional secretary, as loyal secret keeper.

The letters in the second edition consist of:

Part One

1 faux epistle

47 demonstration letters (five were cut out from the first edition's "full deck" of 52 examples)

5 new "love letters" (epistles amatorie) that have no particular passion

Part Two

41 new example letters, some very interesting

Part Three (Office of Secretary)

No additional example letters in this section.

94 total example letters in second edition

Third Edition – 1595

The Title page uses the spelling "Secretorie," which is used on the first three editions. The credited printer is RJ (Richard Jones) and the new named bookseller was C. Burbie (Cuthbert Burby). The STC editors again detect the print work of Orwin on some pages. Cuthbert Burby became the new copyright owner of *The English Secretary* on June 25, 1595, as explained on page 32. Regarding that transfer, Jones and Burby's *assumed* private arrangement is unrecorded. In fact, all these inferential "back-room" sales lack documentation. What we have are those occasions when the new Stationer-owner of a text took the trouble to spend sixpence and re-copyright the book in his own name. In this particular case, the Full Court of the Stationers approved the re-assignment. While there are minor revisions throughout the third edition of *The English Secretary,* the basic structure mirrors the 1592/93 edition. The example letters are the same as in the previous edition, and total 94.

Fourth Edition – 1599

The title page uses the modern spelling, "Secretary," for the first time, and this pattern is followed on all subsequent editions. The credited printer is PS (Peter Short) and the named bookseller was again C. Burbie (Cuthbert Burby). **Peter Short** was an active printer in London in the years 1590 to 1603. Among his work — in the smaller window of 1595-99 — Peter Short printed four works we know as "Shakespeare's," two plays and two of poems, but the plays were offered anonymously. His first was the **anonymous** *Henry VI Part 3,* (First Quarto) in 1595. Next, he printed the **anonymous** *Henry IV, Part 1,* (First Quarto) in two separate editions in 1598. Short also printed the long-awaited second quarto of *Rape of Lucrece,* in 1598. In 1599 Short printed the Q5 of the popular *Venus and Adonis.* Try to keep this all in your mind at the same time: In 1599 the publisher and owner of *The English Secretary* was Cuthbert Burby, who published the anonymous *Romeo and Juliet* Q2, (revised and improved by its anonymous author), that same year. His 1599 *English Secretary* printer was Peter Short, who had published two anonymous (Shakespeare) plays and now had the contract to get the two long poems back in print. In the middle of this is Day, who was still updating his book, and Oxford who was still the named sponsor and honoree.

While there are a few minor revisions throughout the 1599 *English*

Secretary, the structure continues to mirror the format of the 1592/93 edition. The example letters are the same as in the previous two editions and total 94 epistles. After this, all editions follow the model of 1599. All scholars agree that Angel Day made no further changes after 1599 and that any actual differences are printer glitches.

The Structure of *The English Secretary*

The structure of *The English Secretary* is outlined in the book itself with a convenient table of contents. Angel Day's innovation (perhaps not entirely original) involved categorizing the various types of emphasis and tone in business and personal letters. Day classifies the various types of letters into four categories. The first three match those of the art of classical rhetorical oration: demonstrative, deliberative, and judicial. Day's fourth category he calls familiar.

A **demonstrative** letter presents an idea, or narrative news, or passes judgment on a person, action, or thing.

A **deliberative** letter weighs various sides of a problem and tries to persuade or dissuade the reader. This category include loves letters. Day *considers love to be a problem one deliberates!*

Day's **judicial** letters are about accusation and defense. Charge and countercharge.

Familiar letters are among family and friends and include informal business and letters to servants.

This can be broken down further; Day quantifies 32 kinds of letter. I've modernized the spelling.

Demonstrative letters

1. Descriptory—Describing a person, place, idea, or thing
2. Laudatory—Praising a person, place, action, or thing
3. Vituperatory—Dispraising a person, place, action, or thing

Deliberative letters

2. Dehoratory—Dissuading the reader from an action
3. Swasory—Persuasion by argument
4. Disswasory—Persuasion by highlighting negative consequences
5. Responsory—Replies to letters of deliberation
6. Conciliatory—Seeking acquaintance or approval from

higher-status person

7. Reconciliatory—Advances a reconciliation effort
8. Petitory—Requests (petitions) to a person who has something or can do a favor
9. Commendatory—A courteous recommendation of self or third party
10. Consolatory—"Comforting" notes to bereaved persons
11. Monitory—Warnings to naïve or first-offenders
12. Reprehensory—Unpacking the myriad faults of a person
13. Amatory—Love letters

Judicial letters

1. Accusatory—Accusations and Charges
2. Excusatory—Offering excuses for actions
3. Defensory—Defending the challenged actions
4. Expostulatory—Reasoning and arguing a case
5. Exprobatory—Severe critique
6. Invective—Raw attacks on a person directly
7. Purgatory—Unloading completely
8. Comminatory—Direct threat
9. Deprecatory—Humble request
10. Defensory—Defending one's position

Familiar letters

1. Narratory—General correspondence on events
2. Nunciatory—Pertaining to a named person
3. Remuneratory—Appreciation for money or favors received
4. Gratulatory—Congratulating a friend's fortune
5. Objurgatory—Rebuking a person's actions
6. Mandatory—Mundane letters

As you can see, the distinctions between categories are often by name alone; also, most letters, including the ones showcased in *The English Secretary* do not stick within a single category. Nevertheless, the conceit of the book is that every good letter follows a rhetorical formula, and makes use of all tropes and figures of rhetoric appropriate to each category. Scholars of the book seem to take Day completely seriously when he deconstructs each example letter in the light of his Schemes. In fact, once it is recognized that the book is, in no small part, a dry comedic send-up of a rhetorical manual, Day's attempts to tease out rhetorical balance and perfection from the most ludicrous example letters becomes a highly refined form of humor.

DEDICATORIE.

and the inſufficiency thereof the better protected. In which, beſides the continuall manifeſtation of your owne worthineſſe, your L. ſhall binde me to honor you in al duetie and humblenes, praying the eternall creator and guid of all your ſtately enterpriſes, to haue the ſame with your L. in his fauorable protection.

Your L. moſt deuoted and loyally affected.

Angel Daie.

[illegible]

Dedication page of British Library copy of 1586 *The English Secretary*

CHAPTER ELEVEN

Annotations in the 1586 copies

OTHER ELEMENTS in *The English Secretary* are revealing. Of the first edition, 1586, there are only two known extant copies. There are interesting handwritten annotations in each of the two surviving 1586 copies. One is at the British Library and one at the Folger.

The British Library copy is relatively clean. But at the front of the book, at the end of the dedication to Oxford and under Angel Day's name there is a line that seems to be a personal note to the owner of the copy, or by the owner (*at left, enlargement below*). While I have not been able to transcribe this with certainty, I've been helped recently by suggestions from Mark Anderson and Jim Brooks. The second line appears to read "Amicorum pretium .....xiiij." This could mean: "Friendly price ..... 14." The first line appears to refer to a book, with the second word possibly "liber." The words that follow are perhaps a name beginning with the

Your L. moſt deuoted and loyally affected.

Angel Daie.

The annotation just below the close of Day's dedication to Oxford in the British Library's copy of the 1586 *English Secretary*.

letter M.

The Folger copy of the 1586 *English Secretary* has handwritten annotations, almost certainly near-contemporary to the publication. These curious makings, of which I have not found any scholarly reference, consist mostly of underlining, odd "tic" marks in the margin, some words of commentary, and most importantly, for this study, **a series of pointing hands.** When I first saw these hands, in conjunction with the **underlining,** I was struck by the similarity with the annotations in the de Vere copy of the Geneva Bible, also at the Folger Library. [See Roger Stritmatter's dissertation, "The Marginalia of Edward de Vere's Geneva Bible" UMASS 2001, Oxenford Press, Northampton, Massachusetts]

90 THE ENGLISH SECRETORIE.

Epistles hortatorie.

Confirmatio. is pursued. For what hath a man of all that may be left vnto him in this world, wherof to vaunt him-selfe, but the memory of that wherein he hath most worthelye trauailed. The rich reap possessiōs, which when themselues are once passed awaye, are immediatly distributed to others. The pleasures of the world are momentarie, and after we are once dead we perceaue them no

Hypophora. more. Worship, honor, and dignitie, perisheth euen in the very selfe remembraunce. The reuennewes of the mighty, when life is once fled, are no more to be tendred. Shall we then for a nomber of fruitles vanities, (the regard wherof doth neuer last longer, then whilst

Ab æquo. we are in present vse of them) neglect the serch of that

Praise of his aunceſtors. which is of all others most permanent? No surely. So behoooueth not such as your selfe, that of your auncestors haue had so manye good encouragements, beseemeth not the remembraunce of their excellencies in you alone to be perished. Tis *Virtue* beleeue me, that procureth *Fame*, and solie *Fame* that makes men immortall. All other meanes are feeble, as the originall from whence they are deriued is incertaine. At leastwise, it shall many other wayes stande you greatly vpon

A necessitate. to continue this course, in so much as by the æmulation of the virtues of others, you shal thereunto be con-

Hand annotation in Folger copy of 1596 *The English Secretary*

It is *not impossible* that the Folger's 1586 first edition of *The English Secretary* was marked up by the same person who marked the Vere Geneva Bible.

The hands, seen at right below, drawn in 1586 or shortly thereafter, are in a more mature style than the Geneva Bible pointers. But the "Geneva hands"

may have been inked in the early 1570s. We know from our own experience that doodles can change and evolve over the decades. But certainly the differences here are clear enough that this will hardly serve as proof of anything but, rather, as yet another bibliographical curiosity. More study of these marks are required. Further claims at this time would be imprudent.

De Vere Geneva Bible hands

Folger *English Secretary* hands

CHAPTER TWELVE

The dedications to Oxford in greater detail

AS MENTIONED BEFORE, every edition of *The English Secretary* begins with a dedication to the Earl of Oxford.

The first edition's dedication is the most interesting, evoking Zeuxis and Apelles. For reasons we may never fully understand, this flowery dedication was scrapped after the first edition and an entirely new dedication to Oxford was prepared for the 1592/93 second quarto. Subtle changes were made to this newer dedication for the 1595 third edition, and spelling changes were introduced for the final revision (Q4) in 1599. After this, the later reprints re-used the 1599 dedication to Oxford without changes, other than typesetting and spelling, all the way to 1635. While the character of the first dedication is more personal, the revised dedications provide their own insights—and give us clues to the continuing relationship between Day and Oxford from 1586 to 1599. That's 13 years, a long time in late-Elizabethan dog-years.

CHAPTER THIRTEEN

Zeuxis, Apelles, Alexander, Campaspe, Venus

THE ORIGINAL, 1586, dedication from Day to Oxford is the most revealing of the series. He begins:

> **Zeuxis,** endeavouring to paint excellently, made grapes in show so natural that, presenting them to view, men were deceived with their shapes and the birds with their colours. **When Apelles drew Venus** (though the show of beauty seemed wonderful), he daunted not in his workmanship because he knew his cunning excellent. If in penning I were as skilful as the least of these in painting: I should neither faint to present a discourse to **Alexander,** nor to tell a tale to a Philosopher. [The full text of this dedication is given in Chapter 2]

Conspicuous here are the references to Zeuxis and Apelles, both artists of the classical age of Greece.

Zeuxis lived in the 5th century BC. Though none of his original work survives to the present day, we have the legend of Zeuxis as preserved by historian Pliny the Elder. The story goes that Zeuxis was in a rivalry with fellow artist Parrhasius; they staged a competition to reveal who was more skilled in realistic painting. Zeuxis painted grapes so luscious and inviting that real birds flew down to try to eat them. When Zeuxis then asked Parrhasius to pull aside the curtain apparently covering the rival's painting, Parrhasius laughed, demonstrating that his painting portrayed a realistic curtain. Zeuxis conceded the contest; his painting had fooled only dumb animals, while Parrhasius' painting had fooled Zeuxis. To the Renaissance mind, the significant part of the story was Zeuxis' skill at realism through craft or artifice. They were less concerned that Zeuxis was bested by Parrhasius. Thus, allusions to Zeuxis are usually about his painted grapes, so realistic that birds tried to eat them.

While Zeuxis is not mentioned by name in the Shakespeare canon, he is mentioned by deed. In the poem *Venus and Adonis* we read [lines 601–606]:

> Even so poor birds, deceiv'd with painted grapes,
> Do surfeit by the eye and pine the maw,
> Even so she languisheth in her mishaps,
> As those poor birds that helpless berries saw.
> The warm effects which she in him finds missing
> She seeks to kindle with continual kissing.

The Arden Shakespeare edition of *Venus and Adonis,* edited by F.T. Prince, 1960, footnotes these lines with Pliny's tale of Zeuxis through Philemon Holland's translation. But Holland's *Pliny* wasn't published until 1601. *Venus & Adonis* was first printed in 1593. Prince goes on to suggest that Shakespeare might have read about Zeuxis, second hand, through Lodge's *Rosalynde,* Greene's *Dorastus and Fawnia* or Tottel's *Miscellany.* But those are not the likeliest sources for Day. Tottel's, otherwise known as *Songes and Sonnets of the Earl of Surrey,* (Edward de Vere's uncle) mentions painted grapes, but not Zeuxis.

I have found Zeuxis and Apelles mentioned by name in the 1586 Holinshed's *Chronicles,* and North's *Plutarch,* 1579. But **the most immediate source for Day was almost certainly Lyly's *Euphues and his England,* 1580, a book also dedicated to Oxford, which mentions Zeuxis no less than nine times**—once in the dedication and eight times in the text.

In Lyly's dedication to Oxford, he places Zeuxis in an interesting context:

> When **Bucephalus** was painted, **Apelles** craved the judgement of none but **Zeuxis;** when Juppiter was carved, Prisius asked the censure of none but Lysippus: **now Euphues is shadowed,** only I appeale to your honour, not meaning thereby to be carelesse what others thinke, but knowing **that if your Lordship allow it, there is none but will like it, & if there be any so nice, whom nothing can please, if he will not commend it, let him amend it.** And heere right Honourable, although the Historie seeme unperfect, I hope your Lordship will pardon it. **Apelles died not before he could finish Venus, but before he durst.**

Perhaps the name **Bucepahalus** does not ring a bell. There are said to be three truly famous horses from antiquity, the Trojan Horse, built by Odysseus of Ithaca, Pegasus, the winged steed, and Bucephalus, the warhorse of Alexander the Great. Bucephalus, now the least-remembered of the three, has the advantage of being the horse most likely to have actually existed. Bucephalus, in Greek, *bous cephalus,* means the **"ox-headed,"** *bous* being the Greek precursor to the Latin *bos.* Alexander's horse, originally an untamable racer, was broken and trained by young Alexander himself. The horse is said to have had an unusually large head, or, alternately, bone-like knobs where horns would be; thus: bous cephalus. But jet-black Bucephalus (dressed in sable, like Hamlet) had another unique marking: a bright star in the middle of his forehead. So it's not strange at all that Lyly should mention Bucephalus in a dedication to Oxford, whose Vere family arms' chief symbol was the silver star.

Alexander and Bucephalus from the restored Alexander Mosaic of Pompeii, now in the National Archaeological Museum, Naples.

Elizabethans would have known of Bucephalus from Plutarch's Lives (*The lives of the noble Grecians and Romanes,* translated out of Greek into French by J. Amyot and translated into English by Thomas North, 1579).

Bucephalus was a Thessalonian horse. His price (to Philip of Macedon, ~342 B.C.) of thirteen talents has a modern equivalent of perhaps 100 thousand dollars or more. A talent of gold in Greek times has been variously described as the amount that would fill a standard amphora (said to be about one cubic foot) or the weight (or half-weight) of an average man—in gold. These assorted measures do not match, but in any case, *it was a lot of gold.* The heroic Bucephalus accompanied Alexander on most of his famous travels of conquest, dying only at the advanced age of 30 years from battle wounds received at the Battle of Hydaspes in 326 BC (the location is in modern-day Pakistan).

Bucephalus received a military burial there befitting a general and had a town named for him, Bucephalia (also known as Alexandria Bucephalous, or Bucephalon.) Alexander died just three years later. In some mythic accounts of his life, Alexander and his horse shared synchronized life spans.

Alexander was more fond of his horse than he was of his mistress, **Campaspe** (called *Pancaspe* in Greek).

In John Lyly's Campaspe play:

Alexander Now we will see how **Apelles** goeth forward:
I doubt me that nature hath overcom arte, and her countenance his cunning.

Hephest You love, and therefore think any thing.

Alexander **But not so farre in loue with Campaspe as with Bucephalus,**
if occasion serve either of conflicte or of conquest.

Another story of Bucephalus is that as a wild stallion he was **afraid of his own shadow.** Alexander tamed the horse by pointing him towards the sun.

From North's Plutarch 1579: [pages 724- 725]

Then ran Alexander to the horse, and tooke him by the bridle: and turned him towardes the sunne. It seemed that he had marked (as I suppose) how made the horse was to see his owne shadow, which was ever before him in his eye, as he sturred to & fro.

Apelles of Kos lived in the 4th century BC, at the time of Alexander the Great. He was another famed artist of whom we are indebted to Pliny the Elder for details. Pliny relates that Apelles' skill was so profound that by just drawing a single crooked line, his sketch of a man (the crooked jester to Ptolemy I Soter) was instantly recognizable. Another of Pliny's tales of Apelles states that the painter fell in love with Campaspe (one of Alexander the Great's harem) while sketching her from life. The unexpected plot twist on this is that when Alexander saw the magnificent beauty of Apelles' nude portrait, the great general intuited that the artist had seen deeply into Campaspe, and loved her more than he could. When Apelles confesses his love for Campaspe, Alexander tells the artist (in modern paraphrase): "Relax; you take the girl and

I'll take the painting. This portrait will be beautiful forever; it will never age nor betray me. As for Campaspe, I've just learned how loyal *she* is."

Roman copy of the lost Venus Anadyomene of Apelles, Pompeii

Campaspe may have served as the life model for Apelles' celebrated painting of the nude Aphrodite (Venus) rising from the foamy waves, called by some, "Aphrodite of Kos," and by others, "Venus Anadyomene."

Another legend relates that Venus was the subject of Apelles' last, but unfinished, painting. The point of that story, as echoed in the quote from Lyly, above, is that Apelles died before completing his ultimate artistic expression, not because he was incapable, but because he dared not bring into the mortal realm something so truly divine. What the poets sang of Apelles is that he had the power to capture extraordinary beauty through his incomparable skill, and was thoroughly devoted to the Goddess of Love. Renaissance master painter Sandro Botticelli based two paintings on Apelles' work and legend, *Birth of Venus,* and *Calumny of Apelles.*

John Lyly, one of Oxford's secretaries in the early 1580s, brought out a play on this very theme, *A moste excellent comedie of Alexander, Campaspe, and Diogenes: played before the Queenes Maiestie on twelfe day at night, by her Maiesties children, and the children of Poules.* 1584. The Children of Pauls, the top boy's acting troupe, had links to Oxford in the 1580s.

In Act IV, Scene 2, the character Apelles says:

Apel. Gentlewoman! the misfortune I had with your picture, will put you to some pains to sit again to be painted.

Cam. It is small pains for me to sit still, but infinite for you to draw still.

Apel. No, madam! **to paint Venus was a pleasure; but to shadow the sweet face of Campaspe, it is a heaven.**

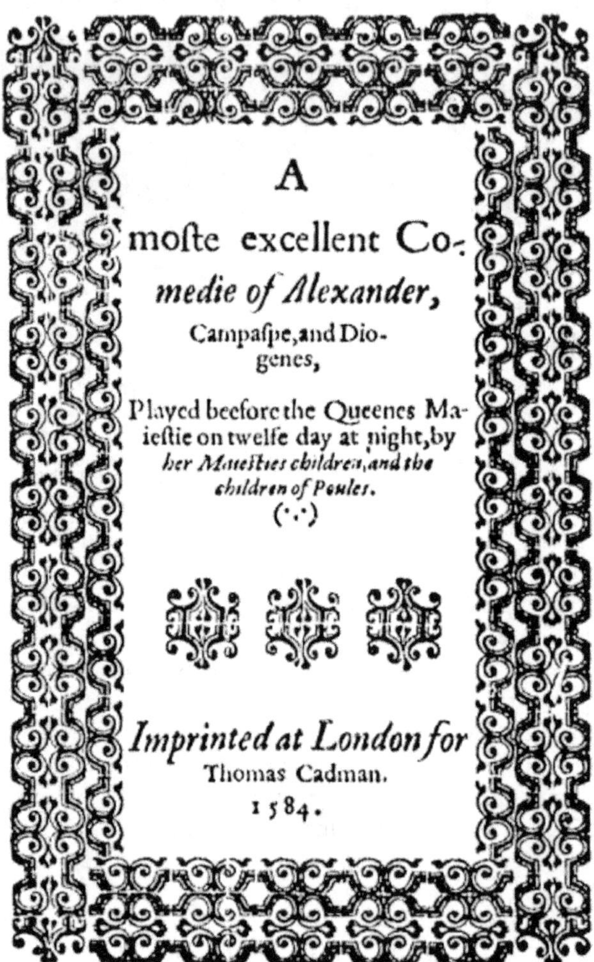

A

moſte excellent Co-
medie of Alexander,
Campaſpe, and Dio-
genes,

Played beefore the Queenes Maieſtie on twelfe day at night, by
her Maieſties children, and the
children of Poules.
(·.·)

Imprinted at London for
Thomas Cadman.
1584.

Later, we read,

Cam. What will you say, if Alexander perceive your love?

Apel. I will say, it is no treason to love.

Cam. But how if he will not suffer thee to see my person?

Apel. Then I will gaze continually on thy picture.

Cam. That wilt not feed thy heart.

Apel. Yet shall it fill mine eye. Besides, the sweet thoughts, the sure hopes, thy protested faith, **will cause me to embrace the shadow continually in mine arms of the which by strong imagination I will make a substance.**

… and …

Page. Apelles! Apelles! look about you! your shop is on fire.

Apel. Ay me! if the picture of Campaspe be burn'd, I am undone.

Alex. Stay, Apelles! no haste ! it is your heart is on fire, not your shop; and if Campaspe hang there, I would she were burnt. But have you the picture of Campaspe ? Belike you love her well, that you care not though all be lost, so she be safe.

Apel. Not love her: but your Majesty knows that painters in their last works are said to excel themselves; and in this **I have so much pleased myself, that the shadow as much delighteth me being an artificer, as the substance doth others that are amorous.**

Oxford used the shadow/substance metaphor in a letter as early as July 1581, sent to Lord Burghley:

But the world is so cunning, *as of a shadow they can make a substance,* and of a likelihood a truth.

Later, the same theme appears in Shakespeare:

2 Henry VI (I.1)

Suffolk To your most gracious hands, that are the substance of that great shadow I did represent.

Merchant of Venice (III.2)

Bassanio Yet look, how far
The substance of my praise doth wrong this shadow in underprizing it, so far this shadow
Doth limp behind the substance.

Merry Wives of Windsor (II.2)

Ford Love like a shadow flies when substance love pursues

Sonnet 37

Whilst that this shadow doth such substance give that I in thy abundance am sufficed
And by a part of all thy glory live.

In Lyly's *Alexander & Campaspe:*

Camp. I thinke in those daies love was well ratified among men on earth, when lust was so full autorised by the Gods in heaven.

Apel. Nay, you may imagine there were women passing amiable, when there were Gods exceding amorous.

Camp. **Were women never so faire, men would be false.**

Apel. **Were women neuer so false, men would be fond.**

Camp. **What counterfeit is this, Apelles?**

Apel. **This is Venus, the Goddesse of loue.**

Here we have Oxford's poem, *If women could be fair and yet not fond,* interjected into a conversation of Apelles and Campaspe just as the subject turns to Venus.

When Day continues, in his dedication, "If in penning I were as skilful as the least of these in painting, I should neither faint to present a discourse to Alexander, nor to tell a tale to a philosopher," he is saying that he is not, personally, in league with the greats of art and artifice, but then suggests that his master, the Earl of Oxford, was in such an "Ivy" league,

> And albeit by the learned view and insight of **your Lordship, whose infancy from the beginning was ever sacred to the Muses, ...**

And,

> I can propose no one in example unto your Lordship more worthy than yourself, who not unacquainted with the special parts and eternized memory of them all, have long since endeavoured **yourself to become a noble pattern of them all,** the exemplifying of whose praise cannot by any speeches of mine be herein more greatly put forwards than the same long since hath been published by the renown of your own proper virtues.

Day is saying that long before 1586 Oxford has distinguished himself as a man of letters, imbued with the skills of the greats and had become a "noble pattern of them all." He also says that his own praise for Oxford has already been "published by the renown of your own proper virtues." This has a double meaning: others have published praises to Oxford, and Oxford's own published work demonstrates his learning and natural skills.

Next, the 1586 dedication also provides some testimony about Day's employment with Oxford, which, unfortunately, is without corroboration outside of the dedication epistles of 1586, 1592, 1595, and 1599, which certainly serve as ongoing testimony.

In 1586, Day writes, "For the shroud of my defence, that have so much dared upon presumption of **your accustomed favour to infix your honoured name in the forefront of this my travail."**

Day is saying, in the language of courtesy, that his "presumption" in dedicating the book was based on "accustomed favor."

Day also says, in 1586,

> **My humble request unto your Lordship is that your gentle acceptance hereof may be an encouragement to my after-endeavours,** for whose sake I know the same shall be of many regarded, and the insufficiency thereof the better protected. In which, besides the continual manifestation of your own worthiness, **your Lordship shall bind me to honour you in all duty and humbleness,** praying the eternal Creator and guide of all your stately enterprises to have the same with your Lordship in his **favourable protection.**
>
> Your Lordship's most devoted and loyally affected, Angel Day

From the above we can draw the following meaning: Day intends to do more work for Oxford on this project, which he terms, "after-endeavors." Day says Oxford "**shall bind me to honour you in all duty and humbleness,**" and Day remains in his Lordship's "**favourable protection.**"

In review, Day praises Oxford and, by association, compares him with Zeuxis and Apelles, both painters so skilled they virtually drew objects into living form. The shadow and substance theme, used by Oxford before his secretaries picked up the metaphor, emerges in Lyly's play of Apelles and Campaspe, and later, throughout the Shakespeare canon. While other contemporaries used variations of this idea (which can be traced back to Plato's famous 'cave' with flickering shadows on the wall) Shakespeare made it into a trademark. The Shakespeare plays also have other instances of art turning to life, such as the Pygmalion-like statue of Hermione that comes back to life in *Winters Tale.*

In *Venus and Adonis* 1593 [lines 289-292], the author ups the ante on this metaphor, resulting in a significant parallel in a famous book, some thirty years later.

> **Look, when a painter would surpass the life,**
> In limning out a well-proportion'd steed,
> His art **with nature's workmanship at strife,**
> As if the dead the living should exceed.

The skillful painting of the horse surpasses the horse itself, as Alexander preferred the reliable beauty of the Campaspe painting to the fickle Campaspe herself.

The poetic emblem by Ben Jonson that accompanies the riff-raff ruffian pictured as frontispiece to the 1623 Shakespeare Folio reads:

This Figure that thou here seest put,
It was for gentle Shakespeare cut;
Wherein the Graver had a strife
With Nature, to out-doo the life :
O, could he but have dravvne his wit
As well in brasse, as he has hit
His face ; the Print would then surpasse
All, that vvas ever vvrit in brass.
But since he cannot, Reader, looke
Not on his Picture, but his Booke.

Jonson is apologizing. He says that unlike great artists, the present engraver has done a bad job of capturing the poet's true face. He has "hit his face"—the poet has been defaced. And by pun, the graver has "hid his face"—concealed the poet. This engraver, called "the Graver" is also a joke, because death and the grave out-do all lives. (As if the dead the living should exceed in V&A.) Jonson's instructions are for us to read the poet's words, not look upon his artificial image, thus reversing the preference of Alexander and Pygmalion, etc. In a bizarre modern return to such peculiar archaic values, many now (apparently) prefer virtual images of eroticism to actual eroticism itself!

Frontispiece, First Folio

CHAPTER FOURTEEN

The later dedications to Oxford

The English Secretorie 1592/93 dedication

To the right Honourable, Edward de Vere, Earle of Oxenford, Vicount Bulbeck, Lord Sandeford and of Badlesmere, and Lord great Chamberlaine of England.

IT is nowe five yeares passed (Right Honourable, & my very good Lorde) since emboldned by your wonted favours, this booke rudely digested, and then roughly delivered, I did in the very nonage thereof recommend unto your L. Patronage. And howbeit at that time, verie little therein appeared worthye so honourable acceptance: yet pleased it your L. the same should then passe under your favourable countenance.

To answer so great bountie therin shewed, I have naught but my simple acknowledgement: and in signification of the will I have to do unto your Lordship any acceptable service, no other matter in shew, then a fresh renovation of the self same title by a second presentment, howbeit in far other manner then formerly was delivered.

Your Lordship may please of your owne ennobled condition to well doing, in pardoning the presumption of the former, to vouchsafe your liking to this lattter, wherein (notwithsatnding the title all one) yet shall you finde the worke both in order, habit and shape, to be diversly chaunged.

To excuse the defect of the one, or enlarge my paines taken in publishing the other, were on either part needlesse: seing my desire in both, hath principally sorted to one self maner of meaning: If your Lordsh. find ought herein answerable to your judgment, it is inough: & the users shal thereby (I hope) find more cause to be satisfied. The wisest of all ages, have not at one instant collected their experience: Plato in his first original was nothing so divine: Socrates in his cradle had not experimented so great wisdome: Hercules past many yeres ere he grew famed by his labors, and onely use and practize enableth unto the greatest performance.

This being considered, though thereout I pretend no warrantie, yet may the respect therof be unto your Lor. a testimony of your owne bountie. As ever I have wished, so hartelie do I pray, the happie advancement of all your Honarable endeavours. And even so remaine:

Your Lordships to be commanded,

Angel Day

The English Secretorie 1595 dedication

To the right Honorable, Edward de Vere, Earle of Oxenford, Vicount Bulbeck, Lord Sandeford and of Badlesmere, and Lord great Chamberlaine of England.

IT is nowe a fewe yeares passed (Right Honourable, & my very good Lorde) since emboldned by your wonted favours, this booke rudely digested, and then roughly delivered, I did in the very nonage thereof recommend unto your L. Patronage. And howbeit at that time, verie little therein appeared worthye so honourable acceptance: yet pleased it your L. the same should then passe under your favourable countenance.

To answer so great bountie therin shewed, I have naught but my simple acknowledgement: and in signification of the will I have to do unto your Lordship any acceptable service, no other matter in shew, then a fresh renovation of the self same title by a second presentment, howbeit in far other manner then formerly was delivered.

Your Lordship may please of your owne ennobled condition to well doing, in pardoning the presumption of the former, to vouchsafe your liking to this lattter, wherein (notwithsatnding the title all one) yet shall you finde the worke both in order, habit and shape, to be diversly chaunged.

To excuse the defect of the one, or enlarge my paines taken in publishing the other, were on either part needlesse: seing my desire in both, hath principally sorted to one self maner of meaning: If your Lordsh. find ought herein answerable to your judgment, it is inough: & the users shal thereby (I hope) find more cause to be satisfied. The wisest of all ages, have not at one instant collected their experience: *Plato* in his first original was nothing so divine: *Socrates* in his cradle had not experimented so great wisdome: *Hercules* past many yeres ere he grew famed by his labors, and onely use and practize enableth unto the greatest performance.

This being considered, though thereout I pretend no warrantie, yet may the respect therof be unto your Lor. a testimony of your owne bountie. As ever I have wished, so hartelie do I pray, the happie advancement of all your Honarable endeavours. And even so remaine:

Your Lordships to be commanded,

Angel Day

The English Secretary 1599 dedication

To the right Honourable Edward de Vere, Earle of Oxenford, Vicount Bulbecke, Lord Standford and of Badlesmere, and Lord great Chamberlaine of England.

IT is now a fewe years passed (Right Honourable, & my very good Lord) since emboldned by your favour, this booke rudely digested, and then roughly delivered, I did in the very nonage thereof recommend unto your Patronage. And howbeit at that time, very little therin appeared worthy so honourable acceptance: yet pleased it your L. the same should then passe under your favourable countenance.

To answer so great bountie therein shewed, I have naught but my simple acknowledgement: and in signification of the will I have to do unto your Lordship any acceptable service, no other matter in shew, then a fresh renovation of the self same title by an other presentment, howbeit in far more orderly manner then formerly was delivered.

Your Lordship may please of your owne ennobled condition to well dooing, in pardoning the presumption of the former, to vouchsafe your liking to this lattter, wherein (notwithsatnding the title all one) yet shall you finde the worke both in order, habit and shape, to be diversly chaunged.

To excuse the defecte of the one, or enlarge my paines taken in publishing the other, were on either part needlesse: seeing my desire in both, hath principally sorted to one self meaning: If your L. find ought herein answerable to your judgment, it is inough: and the users shall thereby (I hope) find more cause to be satisfied. The wisest of all ages, have not at one instant collected their experience: *Plato* in his first original was nothing so divine: *Socrates* in his cradle had no taste of his after wisdom: *Hercules* past many yeres ere he grew famed by his labors, & onely use and practice enableth unto the greatest perfection.

This being so, It will, I trust, seeme in me a matter the more pardonable, to have adventured as I did the formost of this purposed labor, regarding that by a revew of the same it hath now received some shape and proportion. Such as it is I humblie recommend as before, unto your honorable liking. And for my selfe so remaine, alwaies

By your honorable L. to be commanded,

Angel Day

CHAPTER FIFTEEN

The dedications "To the Readers"

IN EACH EDITION, a separate "To the Reader" epistle appears. These changed quite a bit over the editions as well.

1586: The Epistle to the courteous Reader

IT is now sixe yeeres passed (courteous and gentle Reader) since importuned by the earnest requestes of divers my especiall friendes, (more presuming on that they conceived to be in me than of the veritie it selfe, that thereunto might induce me.) I tooke vppon mee in satisfaction of their great importunitie, roughlie to laie out a platforme or Methode, for the inditing and framing of all maner of Epistles and Letters, insomuch as for the confirmation of the necessitie of the worke, & the matter of their demaund, they had then shewed me manie likelihoods and reasons, howe much the same might profite, and how well of divers fortes of people the travaile might be accepted.

The worke beeing then superficiallie begun, without addition either of any regard or industrie to the performance therof (my self hauing greater desire to learne of others, then to become a speciall eye-marke to be noted of all others) as times and seasons altered, so the fancie and conceit therof in me quicklie changed, and the continuance of other exercises for the present more auailable, made me to forget, what therein I had before time promised, whereby the deuise lay dead, and as matter of noe account was ever sithence turned in obliuion.

Neverthelesse about one moneth afore Michaelmas last, the vacation hauing been long, & little to doe, I ransacking divers bundels of olde papers, among the rest found out this formost & for worne beginning, and the Printer as then being by, and perusing what it was, told me also his opinion of the matter, & that he deemed the travaile thereof to be more then thanks-worthie, & therewithall assured me would approue verie necessarie, whereupon his desire & perswasion was (as one greatlie affecting the benefite of his countrie) that I would proceed on so good a ground, and so roundlie went the progression of our arguments forwarde, that it was at length concluded & I faithfullie promised, to finish some part thereof to bee published in this instant terme.

But considering afterwards of the labour, and well perusing what before time I hadde therein done, the order therof so far misliked me, as that I altogether resolved to alter the forme thereby continued, & by such resolution enforced my self to begin anew, by occasion of which, the latter grew greater then before, and I was compelled by my faithfull worde and promise now to finish vp that in hast, which before I coulde not frame my selfe to compasse, upon long continued leysure. Manie no doubt shal you find the imperfections herein, which aswel my self by over-great hast (not hauing so well as I might and would, if leisure had serued me) perfectly perused the same have happily omitted by lack of foresight, in setting the Printer a work, wherby I was (I protest) forced as fast as I could to scrible out the coppy, and to deliver it to presse, least therby he should be compelled to stay and hinder his worke: as also by like default of over speedie dispatch in the Printer, therby misplacing divers figures quoted in the magent, where they are either mistaken, or sometimes not used in those places at all. In occurrence whereof I desire the learned Reader, as he shall find to correct, and the other users therof to beare withal, promising that in the next setting foorth, the same with better regard shall bee considered, and God sparing life with more perfection delivered, the residue of the faults being not manie are in the page after this placed down and corrected.

And nowe touching the order of this booke folowing, I must advertise him that is desirous to take profite thereby, that he first do circumspectlie consider with himself, the severall rules in the particuler chapters, preceeding the orders of these EPISTLES, in such sort as afterwardes they are distinguished, and therin see, what to the better ordering and principall direction, of whatsoever he shall take in hand to write, is therfore for his better instruction enioined.

Next also by diligent animaduersion therof, hee shall the better understande the severall natures and properties, that in the partes of everie EPISTLE, are ordinarily to bee required, besides the use of them in their severall places, and what force they bear, being so sorted out, according to their speciall purposes and directions.

Next for the better inducement & leading the learner into a plaine & perfect platforme of this METHODE following, and to the intent hee may as neere as may be, or as his capacitie at leastwise may any wayes reach unto, know skilfullie & not by rote, how or in what sort he shal happen to do either well or ill, I have first (in a preamble or intermixed discourse, either proceeding or interchangeably passing, before or with the kindes of the sundry examples of every EPISTLE) declared the properties & use of those EPISTLES, upon what parts and places, they and every of them do consist, with what vehemencie or lesse application they are to be inferred or quallified, so that hee who seemeth to have lesse knowledge at al (be it that he have perseverance to conceiue or to distinguish the parts he seeth there laid out before his eies) may with great facilitie, and without anie shewe of difficulcie at all, attaine to whatsoever, herein prescribed, or by the circumstance therof intended to be in any sort delivered.

To the greater ornament whereof, I have applyed such FIGVRES, SCHEMES, and TROPES in the margent of everie EPISTLE, euen with the places where they are used. And at the finishing vp of this worke, have determined in the ende therof (which in the next terme shal as a second part hereunto by gods grace be published) to set them altogeather, and there to explane to the Learners view and for his readier use, their particular natures and qualities, that they who (being unlearned, and hauing a pretie conceit of nuention of them selues) have heeretofore unknowing done well, may see howe with skill and discretion hereafter to pursue the same, and the ignorant also hereof, whose reach hath not byn so ample as others, may be thereby informed what unto well doing is most consonant & agreeing.

Now for the readier finding of those EPISTLES as each of their kindes are suted forth in sundrie EXAMPLES: Peruse but the head of everie page, and under the title of the booke, you shall finde what in the same Page is contained, viz. Wher the EPISTLES be, you shal have them noted in their kindes, as Epistles HORTATORIE, DEHORTATORIE, SVVASORIE or DISSVVASORIE, &c. & likewise in the admixtions, you shall finde, PLACES or PARTS HORTATORIE, COMMENDATORIE, PETITORIE, &c. as they fall out to bee handeled.

This booke shewing these partes before remembred, I have termed by the name of THE ENGLISH SECRETORIE, being in the consideration thereof nothing ignorant what great perfection is to bee required in suche a one, by whose title the same is christened, neither supposing the matter heerein contained to appeare so sufficient, as perfectly therby to enable what in the same function is to be required, but because the orderlie writing of Letters, being a principal part belonging to a SECRETORIE, is by the METHODE heereof delivered to any Learners capacitie, whereout the scholler or anie other that is unfurnished of the knowledge thereof, may gather ayde and furtheraunce, the better by suche means thereafter (if his industry serue therunto) to become a SECRETORIE.

And for so much as this, beeing but the first part thereof, is also the first worke in shew that ever I delivered, I determined as untimelie fruite by occasion of the hastie gatheryng of the same, to put it foorth in common tast, the rather to be satisfied what liking it carrieth. The relesse wherof beyng of the discrete and skilful sort allowed, to furnish a place in any one corner of their banquet: The other part heerefater shall I trust with better liking return, in the after publishing, & to the followers thereof, ryght pleasing and profitable.

Heerein (over and besides the Chapters givyng instruction as aforesaide to the METHODE of these Letters) is only two kinds of EPISTLES wyth their severall partes particularly handeled, that is to say, DEMONSTRATIVE & DELIBERATIVE. The second part shall containe IVDICIAL and FAMILIAR LETTERS, and at the end of the same, the descriptio~s of the FIGVRES, SCHEMES and TROPES, as before I have noted, and lastlie thereunto annexed a Discours of the partes and office of a SECRETORIE, all which God willing I meane by all convenient leysure to performe. Presenting in the meane time what herein set downe to the generall and friendlie regard of all men, beseeching that in courtesie they repute of my trauels, as formost of all other things I therein respected a publike benefite. In affoording whereof, they shall more then belongeth to

> Gentilitie, & encourage me by whatsoever other meanes, to gratifie their courtesie. Fare ye well this fift of Nouember. 1586.

Commentary:

The writer begins with the curious statement that it has been **six years passed** since **importuned** (by the "earnest requests of divers my especiall friendes." Six years back from November 5, 1586 (the date of this epistle, above), would be November 1580. Angel Day's whereabouts and activities in November 1580 can only be guessed at. He was done with his appenticeship as a printer (a career apparently abandoned) and *may* have been a student at Lyon's Inn, though corroboration for 1580 is lacking. Why he would have felt importuned by the demands of his friends cannot be determined. But if this epistle veils another man's interests, we know precisely where the Earl of Oxford was in November 1580. He had been living apart from his wife since his return from Europe in 1576. He had been living with a Catholic woman, Anne Vavasour, and she was, by November, visibly pregnant. Oxford's former friends (and Vavasour's kinsmen) were conspiring against him, and within a month (Christmas 1580) Oxford would confess his various entanglements to the Queen and shortly thereafter (March 1581) found himself **importuned** in the Tower of London. We know that well-to-do inmates of the Tower were allowed visitors and even live-in servants. It is widely thought that Oxford spent much of 1581 writing and working with his various secretaries and assistants. It is not at all inconceivable that *The English Secretary* emerged as a part of this phase of Oxford's career.

The second edition has a revised "To the Reader" dated January 24, 1592—which is our January 24, 1593. This is why I refer to this printing as the 1592/93. Even though a portion of the second was copyrighted in 1587, the date of this Epistle to the Reader proves that the book was still being worked on, more than six years after the first edition (which claims yet another six years of prior development).

1592/93: The Epistle to the courteous Reader

> AS untimely fruite both in blossome and gathering, so untimely spred forth the first part of this purposed Edition. The taste could not bee much pleasing, when in the growth the seasons were so troublesome; yet being borne withall of many for the raritie, of a number tollerated for courtesie, and of some also used (not without profite) for their necessitie, I have presumed once more at times convenient to trie my ability therein, and to piblish to generall view this correction, enlargemnt, and last discoverie ofall that my former and especiall good meaning.

My paines (howbeit in the first Edition publishing) I found to be very great, as well in respect of some hard stormes then casually betyding, as also that being pressed on by the Printer for worke, I was faine to watch continuall nights for his furnishing, and therwithall presently to devise examples werewith to answere every title: yet have I not scaped the common sting of those, who most of al occupie themselves in carping at other mens labours: nor seemed at that time the knowen trueth of the Printers still taking away of the copie from me, so excuse me, in that by want of sight of the matter alreadie past my hands, and forgetfulness by much travaile and watching of that which I had delivered from me, I fel into some multiplicitie of matter, iterating and prescribing perchance besides order or forme, what I could with more leisure have easely corrected within me. By meanes whereof the least troubled with so great a toyle, began soonest to impeach me, and they that hast most libertie to prie, were readiest in their vanitie to winne what they could to disable me. Yet this notwithstanding, I have secondly dared (as I said) to produce this work into light, inabling it as the present time would serve, with the best shadowes of amendment, urging neverthelesse still therein my good meaning, for that (not misconceipted of my selfe) I know it surmounteth my skill. The best natured and not the least discrete, have ever poized in worth, for what profite and of good will hath been tendered. The worst and lesse goverened I reck not of, who either by too much presuming of themselves, or inconsiderate regard of others, mislike or condemne what pleaseth them in the best mens travailes.

If I hit not the marke I aime at, I trust I am not yet so wide but that I may passe for an Archer: Suffizeth, I herein expresse the wish and zeale I have to well doing, let others more excellent give greater ornament when pleaseth them by shew of their cunning. My desire is, if it might be to have all mens favours, but that being impossible, I humbly submit myself to the censure of the worthiest, who because they have vouchsafed (ignorant of the writer) in mine owne ears some of them to excuse my former travailes, I hartely, pray not to seclude these latter from their courteous likings.

This being sufficient for my meaning, and inough of the wise I hope to purchase reconning, I will somewhat speake of the time wherein this enlargement hath been promised, which long since I knowe to have been passed: The respect thereof, not by forgetfulnes, but aswell by the manifold affaires pertinent to my present profession, as by some store of bookes of the former impression remayning, hath hetherto been delayed. But the first copie being now as I understand quite & fully worne out, what by the Printers earnest solicitation, and by a desire of my self to deliver the same agayne in some better order and fashion, I have (during my vacation of other busines) studied as you see to finde some enterchangeable times wherein to performe it. The rather to satisfie the expectation of a number whom I have been enformed to have earnestly looked for and required it, together with the additions pretended to be published. All which in the booke following shall I hope in reasonable sort fall out to be performed.

Now, touching the order and course hereafter reserved in this Methode, I must (as in the former Edition) advertise him that is desirous to take profite thereby, that he first do circumspectly consider with himself, the severall rules in the particuler chapters, preceeding the orders of these Epistles, in such sort as afterwardes they are distinguished, and therin see, what to the better ordering and principall direction, of whatsoever he shall take in hand to write, is there (for his better instruction) enioyned. By diligent animadversion thereof, he shall the better understand the severall natures and properties, that in the partes of everie Epistle, are ordinarily to bee required, besides the use of them in their severall places, and what force they beare, being so sorted out, according to their speciall purposes and directions.

Next for the better inducement and leading the learner into a plaine and perfect platforme of this Methode following, and to the intent he may as neere as may be, or as his capacitie (at leastwise) may any waies reach unto, know (skilfully, & not by rote) how or in what sort he shall happen to doo either well or ill, I have first (in a preamble or intermixed discourse, either proceeding or interchangeably passing, before or with the kindes of every sort of Epistles) declared the properties & use of those Epistles, upon what parts and places, they and every of them doo consist, with what vehemencie or lesse application they are to bee inforced or quallified, so that hee who seemeth to have lesse knowledge at all (be it that he have perseverance to conceiue or to distinguish the parts he seeth there laid out before his eyes) may with great facilitie, and without any shewe of difficulcie at all, attaine to whatsoever, herein prescribed, or by the circumstance therof intended to be in any sort delivered.

To the greater ornament whereof, I have applied a number of Figures, Schemes, and Tropes in the margent of everie Epistle, euen with the places where they are used. And at the end of this worke, have set them altogeather, and therein explaned to the Learners view and for his readier use, their particular natures and qualities, that they who (being unlearned, and having a pretie conceit of invention of themselues) have heeretofore unknowing done well, may see howe with skill and discretion hereafter to pursue the same, and the ignorant also hereof, whose reach hath not byn so ample as others, may bee thereby informed what unto well doing is most consonant and agreeing.

Now for the readier finding of those Epistles, as each of their kindes are suted forth in sundrie Examples: Peruse but the head of every page, there you shall finde what in the same page is contained, viz. Where the Epistles be, you shall have them noted in their kindes, as Epistles Hortatorie, Dehortatorie, Swasorie or Disswasorie, &c. And likewise in the admixtions, you shall finde, Places or Parts Hortatorie, Commendatorie, Petitorie, &c. as they fall out to be handled.

This booke shewing these partes before remembred, I have termed by the name of The English Secretorie, being in the consideration thereof nothing ignorant what great perfection is to be required in suche a one, by whose title the same is delivered, neither supposing the matter herein contained to appeare so sufficient, as perfectly therby to enable what in the same function is to be required, but because the orderlie writing of Letters, being a principall part belonging to a Secretorie, is by the Methode heereof delivered to any Learners capacitie, whereout the Scholler or anie other that is unfurnished of the knowledge thereof, may gather ayde and furtherance, the better by suche meanes thereafter (if his industrie serve thereunto) to become a Secretorie.

Herein (over and besides the Chapters giving instruction as aforesaid to the

Methode of these Letters) be now all kindes of Epistles with their severall parts particulary habdled, that is to say, Demonstrative, Deliberative, Iudiciall and Familiar Letters. And lastly thereunto is annexed my promised discourse of the parts and office of a Secretorie. All which I doo present to the generall and friendly regard of all men, wishing that in curtesie they repute of my travels, as formost of all other things, I therein respected a publike benefite. In affording whereof, they shall do no more then belongeth to good minds, and encourage me by whatsoever other meanes hereafter, to gratifie their favours. Fare ye well this 24 of Ianuary, 1592.

Commentary:

While one can argue that Day wrote this (all orthodox scholars accept it without question) the vocabulary, grammar, and syntax in this epistle are strongly suggestive of the Earl of Oxford's prose style as demonstrated in his extant business letters.

The Epistle to the Readers in 1595 follows the above fairly closely, so I will not reprint it here. However:

The 1595 To The Reader ends with the date: May 24, 1595.

The 1599 Epistle To The Reader is changed again.

1599: To the learned and courteous Readers in generall

Gentlemen, When I do begin first to speake unto you in this action, me thinks, you do espie in me the parts of an ill scholar, who in all his doings, is forced to crave pardon, but hardly findeth the way that may purchase unto him selfe the benefit of such a pardon.

In reformation, two notable instances are held the which as I conceive do crave allowance, though no prerogative in well doing, and these are for a man to find his defect and secondly to have a will to amend it.

I will assure you, though I be not gratious, I would be loathe to seem graceless and this benefit I will have to gain your allowance, that I will blush for mine own errors wher I fault in abilitie, I will shew you my will. And when in all I cannot clear me from your censures, yet shall you courteous forbearance be in me no ways mispised.

I have to foretime as now still travelled with the gardener who first thoweth up his earth on a rude heap, then festereth it, after smootheth it, next squareth it & lastly bringeth it into knots and workmanship, beforewhich you know there are many weeds, loose herbs, grasses, sticks, and rubbish to be picked up and thrown out: And then and not before beginneth his work to draw towards the perfection.

As he, so I, at the first threw up this groundwork in a heap and only did scatter it after, and hereunto I have endeavored to smooth and to square it, picking out therof many things which lay too much disordered. It only now wanteth to be labored on by a more curious workmanship, but because it is my garden place and my provision is too small to perfect on a sudden so spacious a groundwork I will temporize with those duties which either by time may in me be supported or by a greater hability in others may happily hereafter be performed.

Now because it is in all omissions the greatest omision not to be thankful for courtesies I will acknowledge that as you have hitherto beningly dealt with me in the survey of these labours, so have you bound me the more unto you by your favourable censures. And yet, after this continued travel unto this present, you either in mine or in the printers escapes find anything blameworthy cover it I pray you as before you have done with the vaile of your courtesie. The copies before this have been I confess eroneously many ways delivered, and this by the blottings and interlinings had in the former amendments hath peradventure also his escapes or mislikings if any be they are few I hope and therefore the more easy to be tolerated. Only correct wher fault is, and the printer and I shall be beholding unto you.

Having thus performed for my self what unto your worthiness stood mete to be considered, give me now leave I pray you, touching the order and course in this Methode hereafter observed, to say something to them which thereby are to take any benefit or profit. In which case, the learner is circumspectly with himself to consider, the severall rules in the particular chapters, preceeding the orders of these Epistles, in such sort as afterwardes they are distinguished, and therin see, what to the better ordering and principall direction, of whatsoever he shall take in hand to write, is there (for his better instruction) enioyned. By diligent animadversion thereof, he shall the better understand the severall natures and properties, that in the partes of everie Epistle, are ordinarily to bee required, besides the use of them in their severall places, and what force they beare, being so sorted out, according to their speciall purposes and directions.

Next for the better inducement and leading the learner into a plaine and perfect platforme of this Methode following, and to the intent he may as neere as may be, or as his capacitie (at leastwise) may any waies reach unto, know (skilfully, & not by rote) how or in what sort he shall happen to doo either well or ill, I have first (in a preamble or intermixed discourse, either proceeding or interchangeably passing, before or with the kindes of every sort of Epistles) declared the properties & use of those Epistles, upon what parts and places, they and every of them doo consist, with what vehemencie or lesse application they are to bee inforced or quallified, so that hee who seemeth to have lesse knowledge at all (be it that he have perseverance to conceiue or to distinguish the parts he seeth there laid out before his eyes) may with great facilitie, and without any shewe of difficulcie at all, attaine to whatsoever, herein prescribed, or by the circumstance therof intended to be in any sort delivered.

To the greater ornament whereof, I have applied a number of Figures, Schemes, and Tropes in the margent of everie Epistle, euen with the places where they are used. And at the end of this worke, have set them altogeather, and therein explaned to the Learners view and for his readier use, their particular natures and qualities, that they who (being unlearned, and having a pretie conceit of invention of themselues) have heeretofore unknowing done well, may see howe with skill and discretion hereafter to pursue the same, and the ignorant also hereof, whose reach hath not byn so ample as others, may bee thereby informed what unto well doing is most consonant and agreeing.

> Now for the readier finding of those Epistles, as each of their kindes are suted forth in sundrie Examples: Peruse but the head of every page, there you shall finde what in the same page is contained, viz. Where the Epistles be, you shall have them noted in their kindes, as Epistles Hortatorie, Dehortatorie, Swasorie or Disswasorie, &c. And likewise in the admixtions, you shall finde, Places or Parts Hortatorie, Commendatorie, Petitorie, &c. as they fall out to be handled.
>
> This booke shewing these partes before remembred, I have termed by the name of The English Secretorie, being in the consideration thereof nothing ignorant what great perfection is to be required in suche a one, by whose title the same is delivered, neither supposing the matter herein contained to appeare so sufficient, as perfectly therby to enable what in the same function is to be required, but because the orderlie writing of Letters, being a principall part belonging to a Secretorie, is by the Methode heereof delivered to any Learners capacitie, whereout the Scholler or anie other that is unfurnished of the knowledge thereof, may gather ayde and furtherance, the better by suche meanes thereafter (if his industrie serve thereunto) to become a Secretorie.
>
> Herein (over and besides the Chapters giving instruction as aforesaid to the Methode of these Letters) be now all kindes of Epistles with their severall parts particulary handled, that is to say, Demonstrative, Deliberative, Iudiciall and Familiar Letters. And lastly thereunto is annexed my promised discourse of the parts and office of a Secretorie. All which I doo present to the generall and friendly regard of all men, wishing that in curtesie they repute of my travels, as formost of all other things, I therein respected a publike benefite. In affording whereof, they shall do no more then belongeth to good minds, and encourage me by whatsoever other meanes hereafter, to gratifie their favours.

Comments:

There is no "farewell" and no date this time. All subsequent editions use this version of the epistle to the readers. The opening metaphor of the gardener and his evolutionary "heaps" is rather funny. As is the new explanation for all the mistakes found in the previously corrected editions.

CHAPTER SIXTEEN

A plausible scenario

IF ANGEL DAY WAS REALLY the sole author of all this material, and had the exacting skills that he meticulously outlines as essential prerequisites for the office of secretary and the work entailed, all these excuses are pathetic. To this present reader, it seems much more likely that Day was dealing with the erratic, sporadic co-contributions from an eccentric genius. Day was not responsible for the book, nor for its publication schedule. Angel Day was the conduit for the book, and employed to build a frame on which to hang another's elaborate conceit. I do think Day was fully involved and is the lesser of the two writers on display, non-humorous and fussy where the other is expansive, precocious, and preposterous.

To the Right worshipfull, *Francis Gawdey Esquier, one of the Iudges of her Maie-* sties Court of *Kings bench,* and his especial good master: *and to the right worshipfull Sir* William *Hatton* knight, and Thomas Beddingfield, Esquier.

THE sundrie respects (right worshipful) wherin I haue diuersly found my selfe charged vnto your fauours, is cause at this present of my simple dedication vnto you. Otherwise then hereby to signifie either the dutie, or thankefull regard I beare vnto your persons (though it greatly resteth in my will to accomplish) yet is there at this instant no other, or more present profer to be performed. More would I do if I could, lesse can I not effect, without some shew of ingratitude. If I should be silent of that the formost of you haue don, without any merit of my seruice, & conceale the curtesies of the second, by a thankelesse remembrance, and not acknowledge the benignitie of the third, which to me was alwaies vnmeasured, iustly might I of all others be accused, and deserue of each good minde, with small regard to be censured. To shunne the ignominie of these: May it please you, each in particular, to accept of this poore Mite, *wherin, albeit litle remaine worth the estimate, yet is it a signe of good will: And though neither*

CHAPTER SEVENTEEN

The triple dedication to Gawdy, Hatton and Bedingfield

THE 1592/93 EDITION of *The English Secretary* contains a second, interior dedication to Gawdy, Hatton, and Bedingfield. This short passage is extremely significant. As we have seen, the DNB scholars promote this single-instance dedication as evidence of Day's patrons, while ignoring completely the dedications to Oxford which appear at the front of every copy of *The English Secretary.*

Text of the 1592/93 Part Two dedication:

> **To the Right worshipfull, Francis Gawdey Esquier, one of the Iudges of her Maiesties Court of Kings bench, and his especial good master: and to the right worshipfull Sir William Hatton knight, and Thomas Beddingfield, Esquier.**
>
> The sundrie respects (right worshipful) wherin I have diversly found my selfe charged unto your favours, is cause at this present of my simple dedication unto you. Otherwise then hereby to signifie either the dutie, or thankefull regard I heare unto your persons (though it greatly resteth in my will to accomplish) yet is there at this instant no other, or more present profer to be performed. **More would I do if I could, lesse can I not effect, without some shew of ingratitude.** If I should be silent of that the formost of you have done, **without any merit of my service,** yet conceale the curtesies of the second, by a thanklesse remembrance and not acknowledge the benignitie of the third, which to me was alwaies unmeasured, iustly might I of all others be accused, and deserve of each good minde, with small regard to be censured. To shunne the ignomine of these: May it please you, each in particular, to accept this poore Mite, wherin, albeit title remaine worth the estimate, yet it is a sign of good will: And though neither pleasure nor profite were thereout to be collected, yet may it shrowde a testimonie of an honest condition. **Virgil** gave verses to Augustus, but his poems were excellent. **Horace** had a Maecenas, but his wit was singular. **Terence** was applauded of the greatest, but his Comiques were fine. Where, neither excellencie ever grew by Nature, nor witte was at any time

> **ornified** by Art, nor skill should be applauded, for want of enrichment, you may please to vouchsafe a good opinion. The favorable resoect by you hereunto carried, may happiy move this title to be looked on. If any defect be apparent, I crave by your worthiness it may be shadowed. Through the merit to each of you due, on my behalfe, be infinite, I must yet desire you at this instant to be al pleased with a trifle. And howbeit, you have (manifoldly) bound me unto you, yet that the multitude be not wronged by a forced silence. My desire is, rather zealously to think on your goodness, then by any offence of your modesties to multiplie the remembrance. Where much is to be commanded; there needeth small offers to be tendered. The God whose glorie you wish, and my selfe humbly doe prefer, vouchsafe you in this blessed tuition. Your worships more in hart then words. Angel Day.

Note that Day says he knows these three men partly by report and has not done service for any of them. Since, through the book, he is displaying his skills as a secretary, perhaps he was looking for additional employment in 1592–93. Or perhaps this is all a big send-up. After a groaningly obsequious introduction the writer gets to the meat of the epistle. He calls his work a mite, then compares it to the work of Virgil, Horace, and Terence.

These three classical greats were poets, comedians, and satirists. And their stories bump into the ideas of semi-factual fiction and veiled authorship. Virgil used the name Tityrus for himself in his eclogue. His contemporary, Quintus Horatio Flaccus, wrote under the name, Horace. "Terence" was an out-and-out pseudonym. And Horace's chief "epistle," the *ars poetica,* is extremely important in these studies as an antique primer of writing. Though Ben Jonson is often credited with the first English translation of *Ars Poetica* (in 1640), the work was available in Thomas Drant's 1567 edition of *Horace, his art of Poetrie, pistles, and Satyrs Englished...* The book was thus available in Latin and in English, both to Day, and to the Shakespeare author. The influence of the *Ars Poetica* (lines 158-174) is seen as a deep source for the Ages of Man, in *As You Like It* (2/7). Horace wrote, "Ut pictura poesis," "as is painting, so is poetry," which resonates with Day's allusions to Oxford as a Zeuxis. Virgil was the source of Shakespeare's continuing fascination with the Queen Dido and Aeneas story, which he worked into *Titus Andronicus, Hamlet, Antony & Cleopatra, Merchant, Romeo & Juliet, The Tempest, 2 Henry VI,* and elsewhere. Terence's comedies are universally assumed to have served as a general inspiration for Shakespeare's. Specific instances and echoes, however, are all debated, so I will leave that digression alone.

Returning to the point, none of these three antique Romans were particularly noted as rhetoricians. It's a bit odd that the epistle writer, in a preface to his new section on Rhetoric here names not rhetoricians but three of the classic Roman comedians who inspired Oxford and "Shake-speare."

Language in the Triple Dedication

Notice Day's peculiar word, "ornified." It means ornamented. We find it in Oxford's letter to Thomas Bedingfield:

> And in mine opinion as it beautifieth a fair woman to be decked with pearls and precious stones, so much more it **ornifieth** a gentleman to be **furnished in mind** with glittering virtues.

The "*English Secretary* Letter Writer" frequently uses the word **furnish** in ways other than as a reference to physical furniture or equipment. Furnished in the mind. Both Shakespeare and Oxford also speak of mental furniture.

> "To my loving friend Thomas Bedingfield Esquire, one of Her Majesty's gentlemen pensioners." Prefixed to Bedingfield's translation of *Cardanus Comforte,* dedicated to Oxford, 1573.

English Secretary Letter Writer:

> "the scholar or any other that is **unfurnished of the knowledge thereof,** may gather aide and furtherance..."

Oxford:

> "...so much more it ornifieth a gentleman to be **furnished in mind** with glittering virtues."

Shakespeare:

Imogen Thanks, good sir.
You're kindly welcome.

Iachimo [Aside] All of her that is out of door most rich!
If she be **furnish'd with a mind** so rare,
She is alone th' Arabian bird, and I
Have lost the wager.
[*Cymbeline* I, 6]

Oxford:

> My very good lord as I promised your Lordship to send a resolute answer, so now, **beinge fully furnished** for the same..." Cecil Papers 31/68 Oxford to Burghley; 1 April 1595.

Shakespeare:

Lepidus To-morrow, Caesar,
I shall be furnish'd to inform you rightly
Both what by sea and land I can be able
To front this present time.

Caesar Till which encounter,
It is my business too. Farewell.
[*Antony and Cleopatra* I, 4]

CHAPTER EIGHTEEN

Sir William Hatton

TO UNDERSTAND THE CONTEXT of this dedication, it is important to know more about the three men honored by Angel Day: Francis Gawdy, Sir William Hatton, and Thomas Bedingfield. The New DNB entry on Angel Day only mentions Hatton, who actually had second billing at the time, but has now, perhaps, the most name recognition. We will start with him.

Sir William Hatton had been the dedicatee of Day's translation of *Daphnis and Chloe,* 1587, and his name appears again, along with Gawdy's and Bedingfield's in the 1592/93 edition of *The English Secretary,* at the front of part two, *(Tropes)*. Hatton was the son of Dorothy Hatton, the sister of Sir Christopher Hatton. Born William Newport, he was later adopted as heir to Lord Chancellor Hatton and received his uncle's name.

Sir Christopher Hatton (1540-1591) was educated at St. Mary Hall, Oxford, and read law at the Inner Temple, of which he was a lifelong member. It is not widely known that Hatton also had a theatrical side. He took part in the Christmas Revels at the Inner Temple in 1561. Years later, as Lord Chancellor, he co-wrote the tragedy of "Tancred and Gismund," which was performed for the Queen at the Inner Temple in the late 1580s. Hatton was a very close courtier to Queen Elizabeth I, who adored him and elevated him to important government honors and positions. They were so close that Mary Queen of Scots, in 1584, openly accused them of being lovers. Hatton was made Captain of the Queen's Bodyguard, 1572; member of the Privy Council, 1578; Knighted in 1578; granted wine monopoly, 1578; made Lord Chancellor in 1587. As Lord Chancellor, Hatton also presided over the Court of Chancery, and was the sole judge of that high bench from 1587 to 1591. Christopher Hatton had a beloved and trusted sister, Dorothy, whose first marriage was to John Newport of Warwickshire. Hatton's brother, Thomas, was married to John Newport's sister, Ursula. So there was, at the outset, a double connection between the Hattons and the Newports. (For biographical details on the Hattons see Eric St. John Brooks, *Sir Christopher Hatton,* London: Jonathan Cape, 1946, and N.H. Nicolas, *Life and Times of Sir Christopher Hatton,* London, 1847). Hatton and Oxford were close. When Oxford was nearly provoked into a duel with Sir Philip Sidney, Hatton counseled Sidney to back off. When Oxford needed a supporter in Privy Council to further his suits to return to Court, he turned to Hatton. Charles Arundel, who desperately accused Oxford of myriad misdeeds, was held in Hatton's custody in 1580-'81. Hatton sat with Oxford at the trial of Mary Queen of Scots at Fotheringay Castle in 1586.

Sir Christopher Hatton was devoted to the Queen; he never married, and therefore had no direct heir. Anticipating the need for a successor, Christopher willed his estates to his favorite nephew, William Newport, the son of his sister, Dorothy.

Sir William Newport Hatton (c. 1560-1597) was educated at Magdalen College, Oxford, in the 1570s, receiving an honorary degree from the university in 1590. In the late 1570s and early 1580s William ventured overseas. In Paris, he corresponded with his Magdalen classmate, noted lawyer Sir Julius Caesar, who advised the young man to study the Bible as a shield against "foolish popery," and a preventative so that "strange women shall not entrap you." (Sir Julius Caesar also had an Inner Temple connection; he was their Treasurer in 1593.) William represented Corfe Castle in the House of Commons in the late 1580s. William was knighted in 1586. Around this time, Christopher Hatton, who was unmarried and childless, named William as his heir, and William Newport became Sir William Hatton. While he is credited in the Armada pamphlets as being one who served at his own expense, there is no further evidence of his Armada activities. Yet his name appears alongside Oxford's in two Armada pamphlets. Alan Nelson proposes that Burghley's propaganda aim was to show that VIPs from Catholic families had joined the war effort against Spain in 1588. When Lord Chancellor Christopher Hatton died, on November 20, 1591, Sir William inherited considerable lands. But as Hatton had died in debt to the Crown (£40,000, to his utter embarrassment), Sir William also inherited the responsibility for these liabilities. His estates being so encumbered, he never really came into wealth. Sir William did not inherit any of Christopher's political offices so that income was also not forthcoming.

Sir William married, in June 1589, **Elizabeth, daughter of Francis Gawdy,** the noted jurist. Gawdy also had served at the trial of Mary Queen of Scots. Elizabeth Gawdy died sometime in the early 1590s, and, after her death, Sir William Hatton married **Elizabeth Cecil, the granddaughter of Burghley** (daughter of his oldest son, Thomas).

Hatton, Oxford, and Shakespeare

Though Oxford, the Lord Great Chamberlain, and Christopher Hatton, Lord Chancellor, had been friends, they also were rivals, and Oxford certainly found humor in the incidents of Hatton's life. (In a letter to the Queen Hatton wrote that while he was as safe to her as a sheep, the Boar [Oxford] had a tusk that could raze and tear.) Hatton had been the butt of the *Adventures of F.I.* conceit in the *Hundredth Sundry Flowers.* Hatton is widely thought to be the man mocked as Malvolio with cross-garters in *Twelfth Night.* But there's a very odd coincidence involving Hatton and another Shakespeare play. In 1589, at the very marriage of Hatton's heir, Sir William Hatton, to Justice Gawdy's daughter, mentioned above, it is reported that Hatton got up to dance and left his robe on a chair with the words, **"Lie thou there, Chancellor."** In *The Tempest,* in Act 1, scene 2, Prospero lays down his cloak and says: **"Lie there, my art."** (A similar story is told with "Lord Treasurer" as the punch line and Burghley as the significator. See *This Star of England,* p. 542.) However, I have sourced the story back to Hatton, not Burghley. The secondary source is H. Nicolas, *Memoirs...of Sir Christopher Hatton,* pp 478-479. The primary source is a letter from one Captain Francis Allen to Anthony Bacon, August 17, 1589. Allen wrote:

> My Lord Chancellor's heir, Sir William Hatton, hath married Judge Gawdy's daughter and heir; and my Lord Chancellor danced the measures at the solemnity. He left the gown in the chair, saying, "Lie thou there, Chancellor."

Although the date of Sir William Hatton's marriage to Elizabeth Cecil (Burghley's granddaughter) is not known, it must have been before 1595 when Hatton sold Cecil property worth £1,750. Hatton died March 12, 1597, and is buried at Holdenby. He left the Queen a jewel worth £200, and debts totaling £3,700.

For the remarkable significance of the Hattons to the Shakespeare authorship mystery, see Chapter 21.

CHAPTER NINETEEN

Sir Francis Gawdy

THE GAWDYS were a well-established family centered in Norfolk and Suffolk. Their arms feature a green tortoise.

Sir Francis Gawdy (c. 1535–1605), known in history as a jurist, was the third son of Thomas Gawdy (c. 1476– 1556/7) of Norfolk. Like others in his family, Francis trained in law and became a judge of the Court of King's Bench. Francis had actually been baptized with the name, "Thomas," but changed his name to Francis at his baptism, apparently setting a legal precedent for voluntary name changes at confirmation. His law school at the Inns of Court was the **Inner Temple,** which he entered in 1549. He was recorded as reader at **Lyons Inn** in 1561. He was an MP for Morpeth in the Parliament of 1571. After that his legal career blossomed. He was made a Serjeant-at-Law in 1577, and Queen's Serjeant, 1582-1588. It was Sir Francis Gawdy who was selected to open the prosecution's case against Mary Queen of Scots in October 1586 at Fotheringay Castle. Gawdy, elevated to Judge of the Queen's Bench, read out the charges against Mary Stuart and later gave the damning testimony against her in Star Chamber.

Gawdy rose to "Judge of the Court of King's Bench" in 1588 and presided over important State Trials including the trials of the Earl of Arundel (1589), Sir John Perrot (1592), and climaxing with the trials of Essex (1601), and Sir Walter Raleigh in 1603. Gawdy held Raleigh should have bene acquitted. Perhaps in payment for acquiescing to the party line, Gawdy was knighted. He died in December 1605. The DNB biographer, David Ibbetson, thinks that Gawdy had Catholic leanings, despite his family's public Puritan face. **He points to Gawdy's inaction**

at prosecuting Catholics and his friendship with Christopher Hatton. Hatton presided over the marriage of his nephew and adopted heir, Sir William Hatton, to Gawdy's daughter, Elizabeth, in 1589.

Oxford certainly knew Francis Gawdy up close. The two men sat together at the State Trial of Mary Queen of Scots in the Great Chamber at Fotheringay.

Trial of Mary Queen of Scots

Additionally, Gawdy's nephew, Philip Gawdy (1562-1617) an avid letter writer even as a young man, gave us an account of the death of "My Lady of Oxforde" (Anne Cecil de Vere) in 1588 (Nelson, p. 310) and news of Susan Vere's planned marriage to Philip Herbert, Earl of Montgomery in 1604 (Nelson, p. 429). Curiously, author Thomas Nashe (1567–c.1601) as a young man lived under the patronage of the Gawdys of Norfolk, where his father, William Nashe, became country rector of

West Harling, Norfolk, in 1573, hired by Bassingbourne Gawdy Sr., the father of letter-writer Philip Gawdy (above). This fact is found in Charles Nicholl, *A Cup of News,* p. 15.

There is a surviving documentary sketch of the trial of Mary Queen of Scots, in which Oxford, Gawdy, Hatton and others appear together. Oxford is #3 and is shown with a white staff, seated next to his father-in-law, Lord Burghley #2, colleague Lord Chancellor Bromley #1, and the Earl of Shrewsbury #4.

"Master Sergeant Gawdy" is #41 and is shown seated at the main table. Sir Christopher Hatton is #27, seated at the rear bench with his Chancellor's rod, taller than all others. To the right of Hatton is Sir Francis Walsingham #28. If you look closely at this image, you'll notice that only one man in the drawing is shown facing the viewer directly. It's #41, Master Sergeant Gawdy!

In 1592, Francis Gawdy served as High Sheriff of Norfolk. Curiously, in one of the example letters in The English Secretary, the framing conceit is a letter from a nobleman to another man who is seeking election or selection for the high office of County Sheriff. The writer seems to be offering his support for the selection in return for offering his servant, the bearer of the letter, the position of new under-Sheriff.

CHAPTER TWENTY

Thomas Bedingfield

THOMAS BEDINGFIELD (c. 1540s–1613) was referred to by both Oxford and Day as "Esquire," though no law school affiliation has been substantiated. It is reasoned that the Esquire was appropriate to his new position, circa 1572, as a gentleman pensioner to Queen Elizabeth. It is possible that Bedingfield was being rewarded by the Queen in remembrance of the unexpected kindness of Thomas' father, Henry Bedingfield, to her during the reign of her older sister, Mary I. Sir Henry Bedingfield of Norfolk was the new Constable in May 1554, and was dispatched to fetch up young Elizabeth from the Tower of London. Initially, she was apprehensive and terrified of this man, and feared execution. But he took her to Woodstock where he was her keeper for a year. Although he was strict, he was kind to Elizabeth. Thomas Bedingfield was also born in Norfolk, as the second son of Sir Henry Bedingfield (c. 1509–1583), described above. His mother was **Katherine Townshend** (d. 1581), daughter of **Sir Roger Townshend** of Raynham, Norfolk. Oxford sold Castle Rising in 1578 to Roger Townshend (and Robert Buxton). Townshend gave testimony about the Oxford-Knyvet brush-up in 1582. Oxford sold his beloved manor of Wivenhoe to Roger Townshend in 1584. A well-known Catholic family, other members of the Bedingfields are named in Norfolk recusancy records, though Thomas is not; he followed the Church of England, which perhaps smoothed his rise at Court. In the late 1560s Bedingfield arrived in London and, in the words of the new DNB,

> Bedingfield came under the notice of Edward de Vere, the earl of Oxford, to whom he dedicated Cardanus Comforte, Translated into English (1573), his translation of the social and spiritual handbook by Girolamo Cardano, the Italian mathematician. According to the dedication (dated 1572) de Vere commissioned the translation despite Bedingfield's doubts over "my long discontinuance of study" (Cardano, sig. A2r). In a printed reply to this dedication de Vere was pleased that the book showed how "it ornifyeth a gentleman to be furnished in mynde wyth glittering virtues" (ibid., sig. A3v). [L. G. Kelly, "Bedingfield, Thomas," Oxford Dictionary of National Biography, Oxford University Press, Sept 2004]

Bedingfield also translated, in 1588, Machiavelli's *The Florentine Historie,* though the book was not published until 1595. However, the book retains its original dedication to Sir Christopher Hatton (who died in 1591). Thus, Bedingfield is connected to Oxford many ways: they were in a Tournament together in 1571. When Oxford left England, "AWOL," in 1574, Bedingfield was one of the Gentlemen pensioners sent by the Queen to get him back. He is linked to Oxford through the Earl's direct patronage of *Cardanus Comfort* and their dovetailed letters, published in that volume. They are again linked through Oxford's dealings with Bedingfield's father-in-law, Sir Roger Townshend, through Day, who says in the above dedication that he knows Bedingfield ["the benignitie of the third, which to me was alwaies unmeasured"], and through the Hattons, who were loyal friends to the de Veres. Later, King James I appointed Thomas Bedingfield as "master of tents, pavilions, and hale" in 1603, and he lived on to 1613.

CHAPTER TWENTY ONE

The Hatton—Underhill—New Place link

THE MULTIPLE LINKS between the 17th Earl of Oxford and Sir William Hatton may emerge as central in developing a credible solution to the Shakespeare authorship question. It must be stated at the outset that the central facts of the Hatton-Underhill relationship were discovered by researcher Nina Green in 1993 and published in her *Edward de Vere Newsletter #39.* Yet, these facts have remained obscure. It is my hope that by adding new and relevant information to this matter, I can re-launch this particular line of argument.

Simply put, Sir William Hatton's mother, Dorothy Hatton, the Lord Chancellor's sister, had married, secondly, a well-to-do attorney of the Inner Temple and a landowner in Warwickshire, **William Underhill Sr.** This William Underhill was the owner of New Place in Stratford-upon-Avon (he purchased it back in 1567), and it was his son, William Underhill Jr., who sold the house and property to William Shaksper of Stratford on May 4, 1597. The multiple links between the 17th Earl of Oxford and the Hatton family, established long before the sale of New Place to Shakespeare of Stratford, provide a context in which we may begin to understand the mechanics of one crucial piece of the authorship cover-up. The links provided by Oxford's secretary, Angel Day, to Hatton, Gawdy and Bedingfield only serve to further cement these relationships. To state the case even more directly, **William Shaksper of Stratford-upon-Avon purchased New Place in 1597 from William Underhill Jr., who was step-brother to Sir William Hatton, who was married to Lord Treasurer Burghley's grand-daughter, and thus an in-law of Oxford as well as co-dedicatee in *The English Secretary.*** Here are the specific details.

William Underhill Senior of Idlicote, Warwickshire, lived c. 1512–May 31, 1570. Idlicote is a small village about eight miles south of Stratford-upon-Avon. His wife was Ursula Congreve (c. 1515–1561). His eldest son, William Underhill Jr. (c. 1530–July 13, 1597) was the man who sold New Place to Shakespeare of Stratford. The Underhills were not just some country family; their descent from Gilbert de Clare, a signer of the Magna Carta, made them distant relatives of the de Veres. William Underhill Sr. was a lawyer of the Inner Temple and Clerk of Assizes at Warwick. Justice Gawdy was also from the Inner Temple. And, as we have seen, the Inner Temple was the controlling senior institution to Lyons Inn, Angel Day's school. Underhill Sr. first bought property in Barton-on- Heath, an obscure town mentioned in *Taming of the Shrew* as "Burton Heath," the hometown of Sly.

> *Sly* What, would you make me mad? Am not I Christopher Sly, old Sly's son of Burton Heath; by birth a pedlar, by education a cardmaker, by transmutation a bear-herd, and now by present profession a tinker? Ask Marian Hacket, the fat ale-wife of Wincot, if she know me not; if she say I am not fourteen pence on the score for sheer ale, score me up for the lying'st knave in Christendom...[*Taming of the Shrew* I.2]

A chart, right, visualizes the connections between Oxford, the Hattons, Cecils, Gawdys, and Underhills.

When Underhill bought New Place from William Clopton in 1567, Clopton was out of the way in Italy, and Underhill's purchase of the deed, through the unscrupulous William Bott, is slightly clouded, as Underhill took repeated actions against Bott in other circumstances. (see Brassington, *Shakespeare's Homeland,* pp 269 ff). In a bizarre echo of Diogenes, the Stratford Corporation in 1565 expelled Bott as alderman for saying that "there was never an honest man of the Council or body of the corporation of Stratford." (see Schoenbaum, *William Shakespeare, A Documentary Life,* p 173). Next, Underhill bought the manors of Idlicote and Loxley. He married Dorothy Hatton sometime between 1565 and 1570. This time window is spanned by the date of the death of John Newport in 1565 (Dorothy Hatton's first husband) and the date of death of William Underhill, May 31, 1570. His estates passed to his eldest son, William Jr. (c.1530 - July 13, 1597).

The May 4, 1597, deed of sale from Underhill Jr. to "Willielmum Shakespeare" notes a payment of £60 in silver. Schoenbaum considers £60 to be a low figure for the value of the property at the time but also notes that the amounts logged in bills of sale were often "fictional" and the real figure of Shakespeare's out-of-pocket for New Place is unknown. Standard scholars assert that Shakespeare spent all he had on the deal, as he was cited for defaulting on taxes owed in Stratford in November 1597.

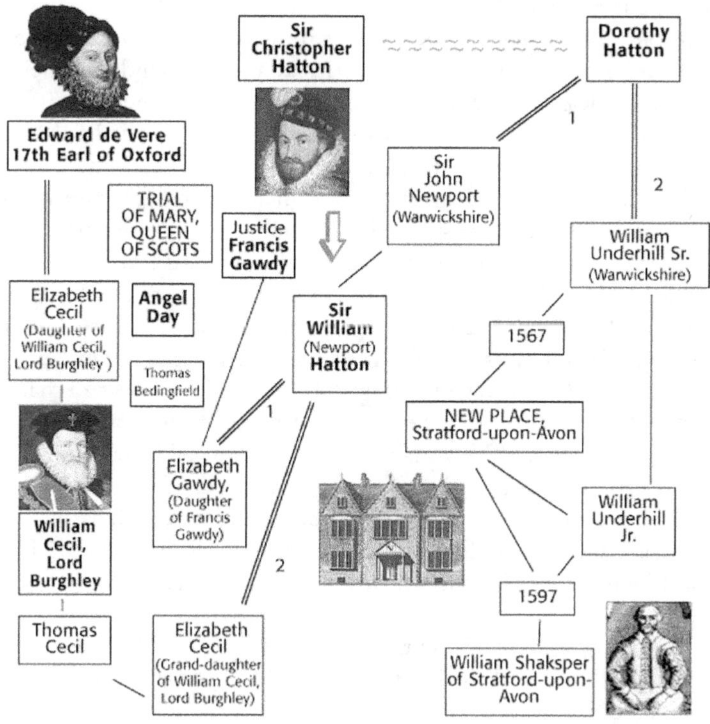

Connections between Oxford, the Hattons, Cecils, Gawdys, and Underhills.

What is known for certain is that almost immediately everything about the sale went sour. **Just two months after selling New Place to W. Shakespeare, William Underhill Jr. was dead,** and foul play via poison was suggested. Suspicion hinged on William Jr.'s son, Fulke Underhill, and, in fact, Fulke Underhill was executed for murdering his father (hanged at Warwick), two years later in the winter of 1598-'99. **As Fulke**

was heir, and accused of murder in 1597, all the Underhill properties reverted to the Crown. Because the sale of New Place had come so close to the death of William Underhill Jr., the title to the Stratford house was also escrowed. Yes, not only was "Shakespeare's New Place" bought from the stepson of Dorothy Hatton (sister of the Lord Chancellor), but Queen Elizabeth herself (as England's chief landlord) was technically the owner of New Place from July 1597 to 1602! Because of the assorted rivalries and treacheries among the Underhill heirs, the transfer of clear ownership to Shakespeare wasn't finalized until 1602, when surviving brother Hercules Underhill finally turned 21 and title to the Underhill estates reverted back from the Crown to the Underhills of Warwickshire. Hercules thereafter signed a new agreement (called a "fine") to William Shakespeare in 1602 that cleared the title to New Place. The house, as Shakespeare received it, was said to be the "second largest house" in Stratford, appropriate for the man who willed his wife his second-best bed. The house came with two barns and two orchards. New Place had no less than ten fireplaces (duly noted because each one was taxed). At the time, while country manors might have had that many hearths, ten fireplaces in a house in the center of a rural town usually meant one thing: that New Place served as an inn, a hostelry, or a brothel.

Even without clear title, Shakespeare of Stratford may have starting living at New Place after the summer of 1597. In Richard Quiney's "Note of Corn and Malt" dated February 4, 1598, Shakespeare is listed as a resident of the Chapel Street ward, which is the appropriate district for New Place.

Adding to the odd chronology of the New Place sale was the sudden death of Sir William Hatton in 1597 that may have precipitated the chain of events.

- March 12, 1597—Sir William Hatton (stepson of William Underhill Sr. and in-law to the Cecils & Veres) dies.

- May 4, 1597—W. Underhill Jr. sells New Place to William Shakespeare of Stratford-upon-Avon.

- July 1597—W. Underhill Jr. is murdered; all Underhill properties (with New Place) head for probate.

CHAPTER TWENTY TWO

The Scanderbeg connection

ANGEL DAY uses the example of Scanderbeg and the secretary to the Great Turk to illustrate the complicated trust involved in being a secretary to an important man. We know that a play on the subject of the Albanian hero, George Scanderbeg, was performed by Oxford's Men circa 1599–1601 and that a book of that play was copyrighted in the Stationers' Register—and presumably printed, though all copies are now lost.

The date of the Scanderbeg play text copyright is July 3, 1601. The Stationers' Register entry reads:

> July 3, 1601 - Edward Allde - the true historye of GEORGE SCANDERBARGE as yt was lately playd by the right honorable Earl of OXENFORD his servantes.

Edward Allde was a well-known printer of that era. Because of the unusual spelling—"Scanderbarge"—it is probable that this is the way the title was type-set on the lost quarto. There is very often a direct spelling match between quarto titles and registration titles.

Further, researcher Nina Green, while transcribing wills of Oxford's relatives, noticed a reference to a Scanderbeg book in the will of Katherine (Trentham) Stanhope (dated September 7, 1619), who, as Elizabeth Trentham's sister, was the sister-in-law to Edward de Vere, 17th Earl of Oxford.

> Item, I give and bequeath unto my said good cousin Mr. Michael Purefey a book which I lent him called Scander bagg.

Notice the way this statement is couched. Apparently Katherine lent her copy (of a book about George Scanderbeg) to her cousin Michael. He never returned it, so she left it to him in her will, apparently possessing a good memory of all her loaned-out books! But as this is the only book mentioned in the will it may have stood out in her memory for a reason.

Not having the book in front of her, she wrote "Scander bagg." With worn fonts and minor dyslexia applied, the name on the play text quarto, "Scanderbarge," may have appeared to read Scander bagge - which comports nicely with Kath Stanhope's spelling Scander Bagg.

There's more. In my Scanderbeg research I found an Elizabethan narrative book about Scanderbeg that has eluded Oxfordian scholarship until now.

That book is called: **The Historie of George Castriot, surnamed Scanderbeg, King of Albanie. Containing his famous actes, his noble deeds of Armes, and memorable victories against the Turkes, for the faith of Christ. Comprised in twelve books. By Jaques de Lavardin, Lord of Plesses Boverot, a Nobleman of France. Newly translated out of French into English by Z. I. Gentleman.** London, Imprinted for William Ponsonby 1596. (Title page reproduced at right.)

Elsewhere I will argue has that this book has a strong Oxfordian origin, and contains some material written by Edward de Vere. For now, it is enough to know that this narrative history did exist, and it preceded by several years the Scanderbeg play associated with Oxford's Men at the close of the 16th century.

George Scanderbeg

Who was Scanderbeg?

While the name "Scanderbeg" does not ring a bell to modern ears, the 15th-century Scanderbeg was a well known heroic figure throughout 15th- and 16th-century Christendom as he had overcome great adversity to become a fearless and heroic defender of Europe against the Turks. His special talents were enhanced by his having grown up at the Court of the Ottoman Sultan where he was trained in Ottoman military strategy.

THE

HISTORIE

OF GEORGE CAS-
TRIOT, SVRNAMED SCAN-
DERBEG, KING OF ALBANIE.

Containing his famous actes, his noble deedes of Armes, and memorable victories againſt the Turkes, for the Faith of Chriſt.

Compriſed in twelue Bookes: By IAQVES DE LAVARDIN, Lord of PLESSIS BOVRROT, a Nobleman of France.

Newly tranſlated out of French into Engliſh by Z. I. Gentleman.

LONDON,
Imprinted for VVilliam Ponſonby.
1596.

Title page, *History of George Castriot, Surnamed Scanderbeg*

The Ottoman Turks invaded Albania in 1423. George Castriot, a young Roman- nosed Caucasian Albanian, son of a local politician, was captured with his family and became a well-kept hostage in the Ottoman Court. For a time he became an authentic Muslim (though he later claimed he was always a Christian in his heart) and grew up to be a military commander of awesome power, defending the Turks against invading armies of Persians, Scythians, and even Christians!

In addition to his family name, Albanian hero George Castriot earned the epithet "Iskander Bey" (Prince Alexander) which became "Scander Beg" in his native tongue in honor of his military abilities. Scanderbeg conquered new territory (Nicomedia and Brusa) for the Sultan Amurath and those Middle Eastern cities were added to the Ottoman empire. Nevertheless, he increasingly risked the betrayal of jealous officers who distrusted him. He was a European after all, and on a fast track in the Ottoman armies. Further, Scanderbeg developed an attack of conscience—a recurring memory of both his family and his former Christianity—and decided to betray the Turks and reclaim his homeland. One of his eventual allies was Alfonso King of Aragon, (the subject of yet another anonymous Elizabethan play). After the pivotal events of his escape back to Albania around 1443 (detailed below) the rest of Scanderbeg's life was spent repelling repeated Turkish invasions—annually, for 25 years until his death in 1468.

E. A. J. Honigmann (*Review of English Studies #174*) posited a thematic link between the legend of Scanderbeg and *Othello.* Young Scanderbeg, as a renegade Christian and de facto Moslem, led Turkish armies against Christian forces while defending the Sultanate. Othello, a Christianized Moslem, led Christian armies against the Turks. When Scanderbeg returned to defend his homeland, he, like Othello, was a "Christianized Moslem," who led Christian armies against the Turks.

Scanderbegging the Question

There is the possibility that one line of the lost play of Oxford's Men has been retained. Dekker's fabulous satire Satiro-Mastix (1602), which contains jokes about many current and recent London plays, has the following line:

> Tuc: Nay, whir, nymble Prickshaft; whir, away, I goe upon life and death, away, flie Scanderbag flie.

Dekker's spelling "Scanderbag" reinforces the idea that he is quoting a line from the play; plus, he uses the same gimmick to send up other plays.

Due diligence requires discussing the "Marlowe" situation. Various sources claim confidently that "Scanderbeg" is a lost play by Christopher Marlowe. But such attribution rests entirely on the interpretation of a single source, Gabriel Harvey's *A New Letter of Notable Contents. With a straunge Sonet, intituled GORGON, Or the wonderfull yeare*. London. 1593. [*New Letter* was the last book published by Harvey.]

Harvey wrote *Peirce's Supererogation* in 1593, an invective against Thomas Nashe. He followed with the small book named above, which contains the Gorgon sonnet sequence that ends the book. These poems are so archly written, so obscure, that "Gorgon" is capable of widely divergent interpretations. For some time the theme of the Sonnet was thought to be a good riddance to Marlowe, who was murdered on May 30, 1593. This interpretation began with A.H. Bullen's *Works of Marlowe* in 1884. He was followed by Grosart and Fleay. But this view began to crumble in the 20th century when R.B. McKerrow looked at the problem in his *Works of Thomas Nashe,* 1904. After much study, McKerrow said of the Gorgon sequence that, "I can only say that it was doubtless intended to have some meaning, but that I have in vain attempted to discover what it may be." Bullen, et al, thought Harvey considered Marlowe to be both a kind of Tamberlaine and a Scanderbag, but Harvey does not say anything explicitly. The OED cites Harvey's use of scanderbegging as a generic insult. Here is the relevant quote from Harvey, 1593:

I mus'd awhile, and, having mus'd a while,
Jesu, (quoth I) *is that* Gargantua minde
Conquerd, and left no Scanderbeg *behinde?*
Vowed he not to Powles a Second bile?
What bile or kibe? *(quoth that same early Spright)*
Have you forgot the Scanderbegging wight?

At present, the arguments regarding the identity of Harvey's "Scanderbegging wight" (among the handful of academics who care about such things) fall into three roughly equal camps: 1) it was Marlowe; 2) it was Nashe; 3) Harvey's wight cannot be determined. Since the Scanderbeg play-text does not survive, the style cannot be determined. The only name actually documented in reference to the Scanderbeg play is the Earl of Oxford.

There were a few references in English books before 1593 to Scanderbeg, notably Thomas Norton, *Orations of Arsanes agaynst Philip ... & of the Embassadors of Venice against the prince that vnder crafty league with*

Scanderbeg … 1560, and Lodowick Lloyd's *The consent of time disciphering the errors of the Grecians* … 1590.

Next, *The English Secretary,* in the January **1593** printing, gave a new interpretive story of Scanderbeg. This book was dedicated to Oxford, and has the second dedication inside to Gawdy, Hatton and Bedingfield. Harvey wrote his Scanderbeg allusions in late 1593. Might not *The English Secretary* have been his immediate source?

The play itself has no chronological footprint that would suggest Marlowe to be the author. It is most likely that the Scanderbeg play of Oxford's Men was a new play circa 1600, (as evidenced by Dekker's 1602 topical allusion, above, and another in his *Shoemakers Holiday* 1600, "no, we have beene bargaining with Skellum Skanderbag," and a quip in Jonson's *Every Man In His Humor,* 1600, "horson scander-hag rogue"). Also, the first comprehensive history of Scanderbeg in English wasn't published until 1596 (see above) and, further, 1600-'01 was the year of a very colorful embassy of Moroccans from the Barbary Coast to London.

Hailed as "The King of the Barbarians," (Barbary Coast), and with the colorful name of "Muley Hamets," this exotic general had been so inspired by the Cadiz raid of the Earl of Essex (1597) that he now secretly proposed to Elizabeth that she form a military alliance with Barbary to invade and conquer Spain once and for all. Although this concept had some interest at court it was rejected because an alliance with infidels was out of the question and occupying and holding Spain would have been an impossible task. Spain would have defaulted back to Muslim control in no time. Also, France would become more powerful as it filled the Spanish vacuum and rallied a crusade against New Grenada. The whole plan was *no bueno.* So Elizabeth instead met with the turbaned counselors to negotiate the release of English hostages in various countries. Not much has changed in 400 years!

This story of Scanderbeg and the secretary to the Great Turk may be entirely forgotten in the modern world (outside of Albania) but in the English Renaissance, Scanderbeg was a popular hero of legend and the story of his dramatic break with the Turks (which hinges on a secretary and forged letters), was known to educated readers, and apparently to a wider audience through a popular stage play unique to Oxford's Men.

Returning to *The English Secretary,* the gratuitous inclusion of the Scanderbeg story in 1592/93 argues for Day's continued professional connection with the Earl of Oxford. It also shows that Oxford and his household were aware of Scanderbeg well before the popular book appeared, and years before the play by Oxford's Men. This illustrative tale of Scanderbeg was first offered in *The English Secretary* in its 1592/93 expanded edition, again in 1595, and then updated for the final revision of 1599.

The tale, as told in *The English Secretary* over several pages, is a bit hard to follow if one does not know the story. My following retelling is based on *The English Secretary* version, and informed by a more modern book, *George Castriot, Surnamed Scanderbeg, King of Albania,* by Clement Clarke Moore, Appleton & Co., 1850.

George Castriot Scanderbeg, once just an outlander hostage, rose through the ranks to become a trusted general in the vast Ottoman military-industrial complex. He gradually planned an escape and revenge. Scanderbeg shared his plans with a small group of trusted family and friends. While on campaign (at Nish on the Morava River) with the Sultan's army against Christian Hungarians led by John Hunyady, Scanderbeg saw his chance. He had been closely watching a man who was the principal Secretary to the Great Turk Belerby of Roumelia who was accompanying the army.

At an opportune moment, Scanderbeg and his select allies leapt upon the Turkish guard who protected the Secretary, and killed them all. Scanderbeg then bound, chained, and imprisoned the Secretary, and by extreme threats forced him to pen letters of safe conduct, as if from the Great Turk himself. The Secretary carried the great seal of the Great Turk, and Ottoman practicedemanded that a letter sealed in this fashion be obeyed without question. A false letter was written to the governor of Croia (a province of Albania now called Kruje, pronounced "Kruya" and meaning "spring"). Croia was Scanderbeg's birthplace and ancestral homeland. This was his brilliantly counterfeited ticket home. The letter required the present Ottoman Governor of Croia to surrender the city to Scanderbeg's command, as newly appointment Governor!

Scanderbeg had the captive Sultan's Secretary weave together personal anecdotes and authentic news of the empire to lend credence to the letters and add general credibility.

When the letters were done, Scanderbeg invited the Secretary to join him in his treason and travel to his distant homeland. The Secretary, utterly loyal to Allah and to the Great Turk, steadfastly refused. Scanderbeg rewarded his loyalty with a swift scimitar death. *(I never said this would be a pleasant story.)* To enforce his subterfuge, Scanderbeg and his growing band of men slaughtered every group of Turks they met on their way back to Albania to delay any news of their treason reaching the Ottoman Court.

When Scanderbeg finally approached his homeland he arranged to arrive at night, at a distance from the city, and sent a small group of emissaries to the city walls dressed in full Ottoman regalia. His own nephew, Amesa, played the part of the Secretary, and though a European, was so artfully disguised and practiced in colloquia and cliché that the emissaries were admitted and the gates opened for Scanderbeg at dawn. After a few days of "peaceful transition" the forces of Scanderbeg suddenly attacked all the Turks and purged the city, beginning decades of bitter war as the Turkish sought revenge in siege after siege.

It's a terrific story, and the role of the loyal Turkish secretary forced into treason against his will is offered in *The English Secretary* as a moral tale, though the moral itself is not clear.

The 1592/93 version begins:

> Scanderbeg, the terrour while he lived, and only man able to confound the Turkish forces, during his infancy, having been trained up with Amurath, father to Mahomet the second Emperour of the Turkes (for that in the conquest of Epirus by the same Amurath, the father of Scanderbeg being slaine, and his Signorie subdued unto the Turk, he was then with others led away into Turkie a captive.) …

Note the run-on sentence and "for that." It is possible that Oxford dictated this section, as it contains many of his characteristic tics. However, if Day frequently "took letters" from Oxford, *by voice,* he would unavoidably pick up all these otherwise unique forms of syntax and habitual phrases. It may be very hard, even with state-of-the-art software, to tweak out the distinctions between "pure Day" and "pure Oxford" in *The English Secretary.* The word, "Signorie" pops out as it is not exactly appropriate to the languages or locales. When Prospero, in Act I of *The Tempest* [I,2] details the crimes of his usurping brother, he says:

> "… and to him put
> The manage of my state; as **at that time**
> **Through all the signories it was the first,**
> And Prospero the prime duke …"

The only other Shakespeare play with "signories" is *Richard II,* where it is used twice [III,1 and IV,1]:

Henry IV Eating the bitter bread of banishment,
Whilst ***you have fed upon my signories,***
Dispark'd my parks and fell'd my forest woods,
From my own windows torn my household coat,
Raz'd out my imprese, leaving me no sign,
Save men's opinions and my living blood,
To show the world I am a gentleman.

Henry IV These differences shall all rest under gage
Till Norfolk be repeal'd - repeal'd he shall be.
And, though mine enemy, **restor'd again**
To all his lands and signories, when he is return'd,
Against Aumerle we will enforce his trial.

In each of these examples the matter involves dispossession of valuable lands and entitlements that were formerly in the family. Just like Scanderbeg—and the 17th Earl of Oxford.

The story of Scanderbeg and the Turk's Secretary was still well known enough in the 19th century that Longfellow wrote a short poem about it. It is so quaint and powerfully emotive that I present excerpts of it here.

Henry Wadsworth Longfellow—*Tales of a Wayside Inn* 1863, "*The Spanish Jew's Second Tale*"; *Scanderbeg.*

In the middle of the night,
In a halt of the hurrying flight,
There came a Scribe of the King
Wearing his signet ring,
And said in a voice severe:
"This is the first dark blot
On thy name, George Castriot!
Then he bade them bind with chains
This man of books and brains;
And the Scribe said: "What misdeed
Have I done, that, without need,
Thou doest to me this thing?"
And Iskander answering
Said unto him: "Not one
Misdeed to me hast thou done;
But for fear that thou shouldst run
And hide thyself from me,
Have I done this unto thee.
Now write me a writing, O Scribe,

Scanderbeg's signet seal

And a blessing be on thy tribe!
A writing sealed with thy ring,
To King Amurath's Pasha
In the city of Croia,
The city moated and walled,
That he surrender the same
In the name of my master, the King;
For what is writ in his name
Can never be recalled.
And the Scribe bowed low in dread,
And unto Iskander said:
Then swift as a shooting star
The curved and shining blade
Of Iskander's scimetar
From its sheath, with jewels bright,
Shot, as he thundered: "Write!"
And the trembling Scribe obeyed,
And wrote in the fitful glare
Of the bivouac fire apart,
With the chill of the midnight air
On his forehead white and bare,
And the chill of death in his heart.
Then again Iskander cried:
"Now follow whither I ride,
For here thou must not stay.
Thou shalt be as my dearest friend,
And honors without end
Shall surround thee on every side,
And attend thee night and day."
But the sullen Scribe replied
"Our pathways here divide;
Allah is great and just,
But we are as ashes and dust;
How shall I do this thing,
Mine leadeth not thy way."
And even as he spoke
Fell a sudden scimetar-stroke,
When no one else was near;
And the Scribe sank to the ground,
As a stone, pushed from the brink
Of a black pool, might sink
With a sob and disappear;
And no one saw the deed;
And in the stillness around
No sound was heard but the sound
Of the hoofs of Iskander's steed,
As forward he sprang with a bound.
Then onward he rode and afar,
With scarce three hundred men,

Through river and forest and fen,
O'er the mountains of Argentar;
And his heart was merry within,
When he crossed the river Drin,
And saw in the gleam of the morn
When I know that my guilty head
Will be forfeit to the King?"

The White Castle Ak-Hissar,
The city Croia called,
The city moated and walled,
The city where he was born,—
And above it the morning star.
Anon from the castle walls
The crescent banner falls,
And the crowd beholds instead,
Like a portent in the sky,
Iskander's banner fly,
The Black Eagle with double head;
And a shout ascends on high,
For men's souls are tired of the Turks,
And their wicked ways and works,
That have made of Ak-Hissar
A city of the plague;
And the loud, exultant cry
That echoes wide and far
Is: "Long live Scanderbeg!"

CHAPTER TWENTY THREE

Analysis of other mainstream scholarship about *The English Secretary*

AN UNEXPECTED FIND in the academic literature was a well written paper on The English Secretary in business studies was: **Hildebrandt,** Herbert W., "A 16th Century Work on Communication: Precursor of Modern Business Communication," Working Paper #190, Division of Research, Graduate School of Business Administration, University of Michigan, 1979. Hildebrandt begins,

> The genesis for theories of communication rests on the ancient oral rhetorical world with poetics, grammar, logic, even dictamen borrowing heavily from those oral concepts. In this paper our focus is on the latter: *dictamen, ars dictandi,* or *dictaminis,* i.e., the art of letter writing, man using the written word to communicate.
>
> Today the visual and oral has replaced, in part, the extraordinary power of the written word. Not so in the Renaissance. Then, idea movement was oral and written, the latter the medium for churchman, nobleman, or merchant. Thus there appeared in English a seminal work that tried to suggest theories, requirements, and examples of good written composition: Angell Day's *The English Secretary or Method of Writing Epistles and Letters.*
>
> The purpose of our paper is to suggest that Day wrote one of the earliest English statements on business communication, namely, the letter as it should be composed by secretaries and others in the 16th century. We will discuss three points: first, Angell Day as a writer of his period; second, etymological mutations that have occurred in the term secretary; and third, the 1599 edition of Day which represented both a theoretical and pragmatic work for communicators of the day.

Hildebrandt goes on to recount the little that is generally known (i.e., the DNB) on Day, and classifies anything further as "speculation." He remarks that Day's apprenticeship in the book trade meant he was exposed to every type of book, manuscript, and communication. He imagines that Day picked up his rhetoric in grammar school. The unfortunate lack of knowledge of the other facts about Day—in this case, that he learned the skills of Chancery at Lyons Inn, means that Hildebrandt is guilty of the very speculation he warns against.

Hildebrandt remarks on the difficulty Day had in getting his work published properly, in each of the editions, and it's true: the faulty page numbering, duplications, and omissions are astonishing, even in the corrected editions, simply proving that we must not judge the authors harshly for the botch-up job created by printers, who moved to the economic beat of their own technical necessities.

> Day must have received criticism—and well he might—of the 1586 edition. Indeed, he publicly chastised the printer of the book for errors brought on by undue haste and pressures, Day promising that things will be better, subsequently. Little is better in 1599 with Day still upbraiding his printer for errors, but more mildly …
>
> "And yet after this continued travell unto this present, you either in mine or in the printers escapes find any thing blame worthy, cover it I pray you as before you haue done with the vaile of your courtesie. The copies before this, have bene I confesse erroniously many wayes delivered, and this by the blottings and interlinings had in the former amendements hath peradventure also his escapes or mistakings; If any be, they are fewe I hope, and therefore the more easie to be tollerated. Onely correct where fault is, and the printer and I shalbe beholden vnto you."

Hildebrandt, like Rambuss, picks up on Day's theme of righteous secrecy, highlighting the same "key" passage from *Secretary:*

> "The Secretorie, as he is a keeper and conserver of secrets, so is he by his Lorde or Maister, and by none other to be directed. To a Closet, there belongeth properlie, a doore, a locke, and a key: to a Secretorie, there appertaineth incidentlie, Honestie, Care, and Fidelitie"

Hildebrandt also notices that while others used the word secretary, for centuries, even, the OED gives Day credit for publishing the first book with "Secretary" in the title.

Hildebrandt proposes that Day's rhetorical "theory" absorbs two different Renaissance modes. He is **formulary** because he advocates learning by imitation of proven models, and **stylistic** because he stresses (or feigns to) the use of "schemes" and tropes. I say "feigns" because the method advocated by Angel Day in his manual, repeatedly emphasizing the importance of brevity, conciseness, clarity, etc., are contradicted by most of the letters he has marshaled as examples. Either Day did not send his "Letter Writer" the memo about brevity, or Day possessed a serious editorial blind spot, or the "seriousness" of whole thing may be a set-up. I'm reminded of Monty Pythonesque routines, where a very serious introduction is followed by something inordinately silly, which serves as a precise rebuttal to the promised high-hat example.

Hildebrandt summarizes Day's letter writing rules as: "aptness of words and sentences, brevity of speech, and comeliness in delivery." As you read through the various example letters I have reproduced, consider if the writer is staying on topic or digressing (aptness), is brief, and has fashioned all with courtesy and comeliness. In my view, *The English Secretary's* letter writer breaks all three of Day's rules.

Then, Hildebrandt says something interesting. In his opinion:

> **The letters for the most part are pragmatic, superior to the theory section which simply carries rhetoric over to letter writing.** A usable business letter, for instance, is one entitled An example of an Epistle Accusatorie in the state of Coniecturall, from a merchant to the father of his servant …

Later, Hildebrandt, says:

> One could hypothesize further that as more people left Latin for the vernacular, the common man had to incorporate the flowers of rhetoric into his communication when writing to persons of privilege: the merchant, politician, churchman, nobleman, master. Ordinary writing, plain writing would remind the common man of his lower class. **Would it not be to the writer's benefit to secure an aristocrat's approval by using similar devices that would sound agreeable? The many letters of Day seem to suggest just that.**

Several mainstream commentators have written that they noticed a difference in tone and quality between the exposition of Day's manual, and the example letters therein. They make nothing of this observation because they have no interest in considering a possible collaboration between this up-and-coming professional secretary and the master writer who employed him. Such thinking is forbidden. Hildebrandt, like all his fellows in academics, never mentions the Earl of Oxford.

Hildebrandt does not discuss the narrative fictional love-letter section that completes the 1586 volume. Instead he speaks only of the truncated Amatory section in all following editions. He thinks Day got bored with love, or it made him nervous!

Hildebrandt:

> Day gives up on love letters, his last exemplary section. Copies I have read show no more wear than other sections of the work, but for Day the task must have been uncomfortable.

In the 1592/93 version Day writes:

> And nowe the last of all these divisions yet unspoken of is Amatorie, whereof because the humours of all sortes with love possessed, are so infinite and so great an uncertaintie in them remaineth, as that perchance even in the verie writing of his letter, the lover himself is somtimes scarce certain of his own intended purpose therein, the lesse must of necessitie be the precepts of the same …

In other words, since lovers are not in their right minds and do not really know what they are saying or why, the rhetorical rules cannot be many because they will not be followed in any case.

And in the revised editions (where the vivid love story of the first edition has been removed, redacted, or excised) Day tries to recast the subject by saying that he has precious little experience writing love letters himself:

> And howbeit the little experience I have had of some conversing in this kinde of studie, hath sufficientlie taught mee to knowe, that the verie instinct or setled impression of this kinde of fantasie is such a Schoolemaister to invention, and so cunning a refiner of any well disposed conceit, as that with very small help, it thereby commonlie performeth much more than well could bee otherwise intended.

This strikes me as an amusing if disingenuous revelation. Clearly there were other reasons for removing the love fantasy of the 1586 *English Secretary* and Day was covering the tracks. I have not identified the actual love affair (if there was one) that served as model for the 1586 tale, but that doesn't mean that a contemporary didn't work it out and complained to the author(s).

The scholar Arthur F. Kinney, in *Humanist Poetics, thought, rhetoric, and fiction in 16th century England,* UMASS 1986, (p. 23), has the following to say about Day's use of imaginary situations:

> Even more popular than prosopopoeia, or what George Puttenham calls in *The Arte of English Poesie* (1589) the **feigning of a person who is fictional,** "when," as Angel Day has it in his *Declaration of all such Tropes, Figures and Schemes* (1592), **"to things without life we frame an action, speech, or person, fitting a man."**

Hildebrandt offers an interesting summation of his impression of Day's ideals:

> Absent in his discussion is what a secretary does, rather includes who he is, namely, the human qualities that a male should possess. Briefly, men—women are never mentioned—should possess qualities not unlike the gods themselves; fidelity, humility, faithfulness, diligence, carefulness, industriousness, wittiness, studiousness, zealousness, discretion, energy, honesty, care, non-slothful, not given to drunkenness, and a host of other qualities too tedious to record.

But was Day really this sort of virtuous Superman? Or was he preaching from the pulpit to empty pews after hours, as his father, the parish clerk, may have done?

Hildebrandt concludes his essay with this thought:

> ... his originality is in implementing ancient communication theory, with examples, formularies, exercises which students, merchants, even the uneducated could use in their letter writing. That he was popular there is no doubt; his Secretary had numerous editions and printing between 1586 and 1625. He may never have thought of the term business communication, but in some way he made an early contribution to it.

Jonathan Goldberg's *Writing matter: from the hands of the English Renaissance,* Stanford University Press, 1990 is an often-quoted source for Day's role in helping the decentralized humanist agenda. Goldberg writes,

> [For Day] ... a secretary is a "keeper or conserver of the secret unto him comitted." One of these secrets is conveyed by Day's initial refusal to make the secretary into a hand, for the secret sharing that he imagines derives from a master whose hand, like that of Vives' nobleman or like the hand of Henry VIII or Elizabeth I, is notable for its invisibility. For Day, the secretary is so fully the hand (and more) of his master that he cannot be reduced to that role. If the secretary is the one in whom trust is reposed in the form of his master's secret, he is also thereby endowed with a secret that is not exactly his own, but the one proper to his office, which is mystified through the description of the person who is to hold it—the perfect gentleman—in the place of the master. What Day's discussion does, then, is to open up the sphere of the private secretary—the sphere of individualized privacy—within an institutionalized setting.

What Goldberg is recognizing as nascent in the 16th century has evolved into the myriad forms of practioner- client non-disclosure that we regularly see in law, medicine, public relations, management, politics, industrial and corporate secrets, and in government and military top secrets.

Goldberg's conclusion on Day is particularly apt:

> As Day insists, the secretary is "to be alwaies at hand", ever ready to dispatch. He is the speed of the letter covering distance. He writes as his lord, 'in his owne person to answere' the letters he delivers, the suits he reports; he functions as the attached/detached hand. Entirely his office, he is that unto which his lord retires—and in whose hand he may be lost. In that threatened and countenanced forgery, a "self" is forged in the secret-sharing of lord and secretary, that differential and differentiated equation upon which literate individuality depends and which extends well beyond the secretaryship to a modern notion of what constitutes individuality and which is (re)produced (from the start) in the letter.

CHAPTER TWENTY FOUR

The lost Skeltonian joke found in *The English Secretary* 1586

MacMANAWAY, in *Notes and Queries,* March 31, 1951, notes that in chapter three of the first edition of there is a short verse referred to as one of Skelton's. The point of his short article is to alert scholars of John Skelton (c.1460-1529) that another fragment attributed to Skelton can be added to the list. The five lines appear truncated in one of the surviving copies. Thankfully, however, the Folger copy of the 1586 contains the page with the redacted verse and is followed by the original page where the verse is printed in full. When someone complains about an item in a book, the troublesome pages were reprinted and the offending page was supposed to be removed from all remaining copies. The new page, the "cancel," replaces the cancelled page. For whatever reason, the Folger copy, which also contains the curious underlining and marginal notations, also has this "forbidden page" intact

along with the cancel. I also noticed this, but did not note the significance until I came across MacManaway's article. While MacManaway does not spell it out, the complaint against the poem must have been that it was deemed dirty or lewd.

What follows is the cancelled verse in its contextual setting, followed by the full verse found in the Folger copy.

> There is besides Saint Albones a place called Margate which sometimes was a Priorie of Nonnes, and ioyned not farre from the Abbey there. To this religious Priorie belonged a Myll, the water-course whereof, came from the Abbey, and upon some displeasure, or annoiance done to the Abbey groundes, grewe to be stopped. The Lady Prioresse of the Nonnerye, seeing her selfe thus highly iniured, and bearing no stomacke to argue the matter with the Abbot, hasteneth by licence to the Court, meaning to acquaint the king with her cause, and from him to seeke redresse: where encountering with Skelton, shee communicateth to him her counsel, and requireth in briefe manner to have the king thereof aduertised, by his skilfull devise in writing, whereupon Skelton wrote, and the Lady misliked. It was too much, and the king importuned with serious affayres, would never peruse it, why sayde Skelton: shall I not deliver to the King the state of your cause, what els answered the Ladye: But I will have it most briefe, in three wordes if it were possible. The conceited scholler perceiuing her humor, wrote immediately as followeth.
>
> *Humbly complayneth to your high estate,*
> *The Lady Prioresse of Margate. &c.*
>
> Two lines more were conteined in this petition, the conveiaunce whereof being pithie, yet including wordes(perhaps of worse interpretation) then by the veritie the authours meaning might in truth be coniectured, have since the publishing heereof upon farther consideration been thought meete for modesties sake to be left out.

In the variant edition of the 1586, held at the Folger, the full verse reads:

Humbly complayneth to your high estate,
The Lady Prioresse of Margate. &c.
For that the Abbot of S. Albones did stoppe,
With two stone and a stake her water gappe.
Helpe Lord for God Sake.

Do I need to explain the joke? It's pretty obvious, but some people need to have these vulgar things explained. Skelton's jest is that the Abbott stopped up the Lady Prioress's "water gappe" with "two stones and a stake." Whether this is an authentic Skelton joke reported by Day, or a jest by Day, or by his collaborator, is not the real point. The significant matter is that Day, who comes across as a very serious cookie, uses Skelton's five-line verse as an example of a pithy, brief letter!

MacManaway takes the whole incident at face value, credits Day with recording an otherwise unknown but authentic Skelton verse, and credits himself with this important discovery for all Skeltonian scholars. We see repeatedly in *The English Secretary* promises of precise and sober scholarship followed by the most ribald, inappropriate, and dubious examples.

I hold that this comic contrariness was what made the book a best-seller for fifty years, a kind of inside joke among scribes, scriveners, secretaries, and stationers. We can also understand John Massinger's dismissal of *The English Secretary* in 1640 as a "malicious idol."

CHAPTER TWENTY FIVE

The five epistolatory letters that were *cut* after 1586

ONE EXAMPLE MORE SEMBLABLE to the first as well for that it carrieth in it so rightly the nature of this demonstratiue kinde, without intermixion at all, as also in respect of the very perfect and orderly delivery thereof. I will preferre unto your imitation, the matter whereof upon occasion of the ambassage of Sir George Carie into Scotland, was written by M. R. Bowes being there then in his company, to the right honourable L. Hunsdon, containing onelye a Narration of his enterteignement, with some occurrents mentioning the state of the countrye at that instant, which by chaunce (in the writing hereof) among other old papers happened into my handes.

1586 Letter 4—"George Carey"

IT may please your good L. On the twelfth hereof S George Carey and his company came to the Town, with greater speed then the LI. here looked for: causing them heereby (as they saye) to omit sundrye complements of enterteingnement to have beene shewèd to him, both in the way, and also at his ariuall heere. And albeit audience was required to have beene given on the morrow, yet it could not be obtained before this daye, which delaye was partly excused by our sodaine comming, but the chiefe cause appeared to be by the unreadines of the king.

On the morrow after our comming the Earles of Marre and Gowrie, the L. Lindsey, the M. of Glamis, Iustice Clearke, Clearke Register, and sundry other of the Councell and Gentl. came to Sir George, offering all courtesies to him, and good deuotion to her Maiestye.

This daie audience was graunted, whereupon Sir George delivered to the king her maiesties directions given him in charge, with such discretion & good order, as aunswered fullie the contents of his instructions, and sounded greatly to his own commendation, giving me iuste occasion to thinke my selfe happie, to follow one that could with such sufficiencie discharge the dutie requisite on his part.

The king appearing to be partly passionate at the first, did acknowledge him-selfe greatlye beholden to her maiestie for her great benefits, with offer and promise to be found thankfull for the same, excusing still the abuses of the Duke towardes him-selfe, and other unthankfulnes shewed to her maiestye. All which he would have drawn to have come rather by the oversight of councellors, adising & consenting to the causes of the same, then by the Duke, that little medled (as he thought) in such matters. And for his further aunswer, he hath referred it to his next conference, wherin it is hoped he shall be brought to better understanding of his state, and of the doinges of the Duke, as by the next your L. shal have further advertisement.

The Duke continueth as yet in Dunbarton, accompanied with the M. of Seton, the M. of Leuinston, & sundry others besides his owne companye, he pretendeth to have want of sundry requisits needful for his departure & transportation, & thereon hath sent to the k. to pray longer time, which is denied, and order given this day unto him to obey, & to keep the appointment prescribed. The piece of Dunbarton is wel victualed & furnished, & albeit it is delivered to the custody & charge of W. Steward for the K. yet it is in the dukes power to command & dispose of the same as he pleaseth. Upon sundry respects the K. & his LI. have deferred the convention until the x. of October next, minding to have the same at Edenbourgh, & thereby to establish both a good order for the kinges person, his house and revenewes, as also for the pollicie of the gouenment. And thus referring al others to the next occasion, with my humble dutie, I pray unto God to have your L. in his blessed keeping. Sterling the of October, &c.

1586 Letter 10—"Sir, I do not know"

An Epistle Hortatorie wherein the vehemencie of Exhortation is lenified, by a more gentle or submissiue kinde of deliverie.

Sir I doe not knowe whether by the great affection I doe beare unto you and yours, or by some straunger motion of my selfe, friendly wishing to all men, or perchaunce supposing it a percell of my duety charitablie to exhorte, or what other cause you may deeme that moveth me in sort following to take upon me to write to you. Neverthelesse intending sufficiently of your courtesie, I have thought meete in the behalfe of the young Gentleman your sonne, whome with muche ado I have entreated home to my house lying there very sickly, both in respect of hys sicknesse, and for the better remedie thereof hereby to become a meane unto you. And albeit (such is his gentle condition) as from his own mouth I cannot gather the occasion, yet is not the surmise thereof unsuspected of others, nor my selfe by many circumstances am ignoraunt from whence the originall doth proceede. For the better opening whereof, it shall not be amisse to call in question his owne estate, what you are unto him present, and what in tyme to come, you both may, and (in respect of nature) wil, or ought to become unto him. Principally therefore touching his own state, it is yet greene, weake and almost of no force, and by abilitie so much the lesse, by howe muche the more hee hath sundry occasions to be endamaged, namely by reason of his sutes in law and otherwise. Next drawing to your selfe, you are his Graundfather, the onely patron of his succession, and the principall parte from whence the full remainder of his ioy, comfort and happie quiet is drawne to be reposed. Lastly, you are in present unto him a severe governour, and a districte commaunder: In time to come both of your selfe and hys good inclination encouraging you, may and shall be a resolute and setled foundation, whereupon the life following which it pleaseth God to lend him, shall more substantially, and with greater maintenance be led and continued. And albeit in all present actions and things afterward to be hoped, I may not finde meanes to discommend your grauitie, who upon great wisedome, auntiet experience, and perfect proofe, doe best knowe what beseemeth the education of those, whom fatherly care chiefly concerneth, yet because the conditions of the sonne, are nothing such as craveth so hard looking to, and that you may not be nimis durus & perquam severus pater: such as in Terence Aedelphus is alleadged, that would induce an ill disposed sonne clam patre, and as it were in secrete, to doe many enormities, not so much as the sound wherof, should perchaunce ever attaine the curious searche of his fathers hearkening. I would be thus bold to say unto you, that being frequented with so milde a condition as is in your sonne, in whome no ill disposition is found at all, you should so farre forth, yea in all outward shew and common actions (being at this state and at these yeares as he is) become such unto him, as of whome hee might presume, be bould to vaunt, and the worlde to take notice and accompt of, seeing that libertie never turneth to loosnesse, that by nature is charged with so many vertuous directions.

Leaving prophane aucthorities and morall argumentes, doe wee not see that in the holye people of God, the seed of Israel, old Iacob himself, having happily transported his old age, to see the blessed succession of Ioseph, how loving ly he reioyced upon them, beeing the children of his youngest sonne, and accordyng to theyr vertues, as bred of his owne loynes, tendred and blessed them. What made Dauid having constrayned the rest of his children (whose lives he knew) from hys infancy, and above al other, to nourish Solomon, and to edopt unto him, hys princely seate in succession, but vertue that followed hym? What made manye good menne besides, whose examples are innumerable, to geue libertie to some of theyr of- spring and severelie to correcte others, but the contrarye suppose, conceived in eyther of them? But what? doe I inferre hereuppon, that to your pupill, you are not a lo-Parent? no, for that I knowe the contrarye. What then doe I complayne of, woulde you knowe? Forsooth for that thys love of yours, is mixed wyth too muche severitye, you keepe hym too shorte, you restrayne hym too muche. What though, when God shall call you hence, you leaue hym in succession, you mean to do wel and more besides, is that inough? when hee hathe by sute in lawe, whereunto, you have put him forward, endaungered hymselfe, spent the greatest part of hys lyttle, is crosed wyth manie evill practises, martyred with a thousande cares, defectes, and wantes, and hathe thereunto, little or almost no reliefe, supplye or good encouragement, but perchaunce harde lookes, and evill opinion of some, who in respecte of nature, ought to be more friendly unto hym besides your selfe, is it marueyle if hee be sicke beeyng thus wearyed, so greeved, and in suche sorte turmoyled?

I doe promise you Sir, it greeueth me to see it, and that I have so muche cause to reporte it (supposing your owne condition to be flexible inough towardes hym, if it be not peruerted) I doe thinke if redresse bee not geven, and that he have present comforte, assistaunce, and good encouragement at your hands, hee will not be long lived.

Be therefore (good sir) favourable to your owne, in respect of your selfe, and that you are the originall: he is not his fathers but your childe, you ought, you muste, you are bounde to tender hym, to furnishe hym, to care for hym. Needefull is it, you doe now call to remembraunce, he is no more an infant, but at mans estate, whome you have brought çpe to your likyng, ordered for your likeyng, and bestowed at your likyng, because as all menne coniectured you made him your liking, by reason whereof you can not nor may in any sorte withdraw or call back, what you have before determined. Nature, deuine and humaine lawes, common custome and societie, do hereunto perswade you, vrge you, nay compell you. Behooueth not, you suffer that government, for which you are knowne to be wise, herein alone to be blemished. But what doe I inferre thus much unto you, who (farr better then my selfe) doe knowe what beseemeth you? Certes sir, not for that I doubt therof, but because the care I have of the action, maketh me more zealous hereof. The long notice I have had and estimate,

I retayne of your acquaintance, the reputation of your selfe, and absolute expectation of the young gentleman, have thus farre incited me, wherin if I have proceeded farther then I ought, thinke that it is in respect of the great good will I have ought. In the acknowledgement wherof, praying al that possibly may be intreated at your handes for your sonne I doe right heartily bid you farewell. this of &c.

1586 Letter 11—"Sir, I have well conceived"

Sir I have wel conceived of your letter sent unto me in the behalfe of my sonne. T. and doe take verye kindely whatsoever therin with good affection you have so plentifully tendred I am very sorie to heare of hys sicknesse, and doe thanke you manye tymes for your loving conceit towards him andus, in that you have bequeathed for our sakes his carefull attendance to your own looking to, the courtesie whereof, shal neither by my felf, nor by any other his neerest friends be at any time forgotten. In signe that your good counsel hath preuailed with me, and that the weight of your wordes have bene of force unto me, I have sent him a letter heerein closed & ten pound in mony, by this bearer, which I pray you of all loves see disbursed to his uses. You shall also so much intend of me, as in my name to comfort him, & assure him hereafter (upon his no worse desertes) of good expectation from me. For such farther charge as you have bin at with him I leaue to my self in as ample maner as I may to see requited. In the weight wherof, I doe pray you to bee assertained that you shall finde of me suche a one, who will not fayle to hys uttermost to stand assured towardes you. Because the vacation is now long, I hold it not amisse if upon hys safe recoverie, my sonne doe come downe into the countrey, the better to recreate his wearied conceites from his former melancholie. I have appoynted my man to attend him a while that returning back againe, hee may bring unto me, the more certaine and assured notes of hys safetie. Not holding my selfe ill besteade to remaine charged to one so courteous as your selfe: I give you to the protection of the almightie, and my selfe to a speedie requitall. L. this of &c.

1586 Letter 16—"Sir it discontenteth me not a little"

Sir it discontenteth me not a litle to be informed by your letter, of the iniust suppose that men so unkindly conceive of me, touching the ill disposed behauiour of my younger brother, but moste of all misliketh me, that you who have so long knowne me, shoulde with the rash conceite of the residue, adiudge me so peremptorily, as partly being of common opinion with them, to deeme by the naked shew of his ill estate, that the same proceedeth either of my too little care, negligent indeuour, or ill circumspection, in not respecting and prouiding sufficiently what needfully beseemeth him.

Beleue me sir, the conceit of all or any of these, touching what concerneth mine own peculier regard, are unto me most iniurious, neither (to whom soever have knowne me) did I in all my life as I thinke, give anye such token or matter of likelihood, as wherby I might be supposed so muche to impugne my selfe, or to have bene iniurious to any.

The boy I confesse in nature is my brother, deare and charie inough unto me, in respect wee had one father and mother. Howe warie I have ever bene over all his demeanours, how watchfull in the first prevention of all hys untoward purposes, howe willing hee might be trained up in that beseemed his parentes, the cost I have bin at, with him his tutors that should have cared for him, those that have had most doings about him, can chiefly testifie. If I shuld tel it you, you would not thinke it, if it should be reported to many others, they would scarce beleue it. Before God sir, I must tell you, it is straunge and very sttaunge unto me, that being in maner a childe, so well fostered as he hath bene, so little knowing of want or penurie as he hath done, so unwoontedly accustomed to this hardnesse by hym newly begunne, in what sorte he can endure it, & with what appetite he can so grosely away with it.

Witte he hath inough I confesse, but too too evill addicted, conceite plentifull, but most untowardly followed, qualities to be accompted of, but vilely misled, Alas the remembraunce greeueth me to thinke on it, and I would I had spent largely to redresse it. It is neither want of care, love, liking, or looking to, that hath procured it, permitteth it, or hindereth to reclayme it. It is the frowning heavens and his wicked destinie that performeth it. The fire the more it is covered, the more it breaketh out and flameth. The swift currant never so little stopped, overfloweth the threshold. I would be loth to inferr unto you that (by what decree I know not ordayned) hee is thus violently caried. Neither woulde I gladly stand upon these determinations, that the force therof may not in time bee suppressed, But knowing the meanes I have thereto applied, I promise you for my part, I hold it to be greatly feared.

Ths one conclusion may rest (sir) for your generall satisfaction. The boie is nowe neere about you, finde meanes I beseeche you (for the love I knowe you oweus) to winne him once unto you, my self wil be at anie cost whatsoever, to satisfie you: So thereby hee may be redeemed, order him, deale with him, place him, doe to him what you list, or can suppose to bee meetest, there shall not want, to enlarge it, to cherish it, and to the uttermost to mayntaine it. Meane while till you have approoued what I have wished, and gladly would care to bee accomplished, deale favourablye and no worse with me I pray you, then I deserue for your own, and all others opinions. Thanking your good care, and consideration had in hys and my behalfe, I doe herewith bid you hartily farewell. R. this of &c.

1586 Letter 34—"Good M.D."

Good M. D. I am more beholding unto you then I can well recount, for the great paines and loving indeuour, wherein you have travailed about my redemption as I may terme it, which althogh it hath wrought in effect my assuraunce, yet is there somwhat more to be added according to my friendes direction, as by this inclosed you may at large perceaue. Wherefore sir I beseech you (as before) thinke it no paines to make a good ende of that which you have so well begunne.

My request is, that you will now use this discretion for me, wherewith so many times you have stoode me in stead, I meane in conference with suche personnes, whose names herein shall be unto you delivered. Your dealing circumspectlye with them handled (as no doubt you can) shall greatly auaile to my speedye dispatch. Monday is the day wherein I am like to win the goale, which without you I shal never attaine unto. For which your friendly action, both in this, & that already done, I vow to God while I shal live, to be whole at your commaundement, I have sent this bearer to attend you to those places, and therwith my most harty commendations unto your self and your bedfellow, whom I pray you to thank for her courtesie, and let her understand, that if ever I shall have libety, I wil be more thankful, then either my wordes can import , or at this instant is in my power to manifest. Expecting neverthelesse, as much by you to be satisfied, as if there were in me to bee hoped a greater recompence. I praye you sir acquaint not this bearer with the cause, who thereunto is as yet a straunger, and so I meane shall continue, notwithstanding I doe now use his travaile for the present turne. My last conclusion requireth your convenient hast, for the performance of this occasion, in the consideration whereof, I praye you to measure me as your moste regarded friende, who in all actions whatsoever shall bee still bent to the becke of your assured liking, &c.

THE

COPIE OF A LET-
TER SENT OVT OF
ENGL AND TO DON BERNARDIN
MENDOZA AMBASSADOVR IN FRANCE FOR
the King of Spaine, declaring the ſtate of England, con-
trary to the opinion of *Don Bernardin*, and of all
his partizans Spaniardes and others.

This Letter, although it was ſent to Don Bernardin Mendoza, *yet, by good hap, the Copies thereof aſwell in Engliſh as in French, were found in the chamber of one* Richard Leigh *a* Seminarie Prieſt, *who was lately executed for high treaſon committed in the time that the Spaniſh Armada was on the ſeas.*

Whereunto are adioyned certaine late Aduertiſements, concerning the loſſes and diſtreſſes happened to the Spaniſh Nauie, aſwell in fight with the Engliſh Nauie in the narrow ſeas of England, as alſo by tempeſts, and contrarie winds, vpon the Weſt, and North coaſts of Ireland, in their returne from the Northerne Iſles beyond Scotland.

Imprinted at London by I. Vautrollier for
Richard Field. 1588.

"Mendoza letter" book, title page

CHAPTER TWENTY SIX

The Armada pamphlets

SHORTLY AFTER THE DEFEAT of the Spanish Armada in 1588, the events of that day began to be "spun", for political and social purposes, in publications. Thus, in one version of history, the 17th Earl of Oxford did not participate in the Armada preparations or sea battles, while in other versions of the same history, he did. Two books from 1588 and 1589 tell this second, romanticized version of the English victory and its participants.

The first book (title page shown at left) is actually credited to Lord Burghley in modern bibliographies. It was originally named:

> The copie of a letter sent out of England to Don Bernardin Mendoza ambassadour in France for the King of Spaine declaring the state of England, contrary to the opinion of Don Bernardin, and of all his partizans Spaniardes and others. This letter, although it was sent to Don Bernardin Mendoza, yet, by good hap, the copies therof aswell in English as in French, were found in the chamber of one Richard Leigh a seminarie priest, who was lately executed for high treason committed in the time that the Spanish Armada was on the seas. Whereunto are adioyned certaine late aduertisements, concerning the losses and distresses happened to the Spanish nauie, aswell in fight with the English nauie in the narrow seas of England, as also by tempests, and contrarie winds, vpon the west, and north coasts of Ireland, in their returne from the northerne isles beyond Scotland. I Vautrolier for R. Field, 1588.

The quarto has the same design—and same publisher, Richard Field, of *Venus and Adonis* in 1593. In this booklet, the relevant section on English patriots who furnished their own ships (shown overleaf) reads as follows:

> And to shew the great readines in a generalitie of sundrie others at the same time, to aduenture their liues in the said seruice, there went to the Seas at the same

time diuers Gentlemen of good reputation, who voluntarily without any charge, & without knowledge of the Quéene, put themselues into the Quéens Nauy in sundry ships, wherein they serued at the fight afore Callice: of which number being very great, I remember that the names of some of them were these: Master **Henry Brooke sonne & heire to the Lord Cobham,** Sir **Thomas Cecil** sonne and heire to the Lord Treasurer, Sir **William Hatton** heire to the Lord Chancellour **Sir Horatio Pallavicino** a Knight of Genua, Master **Robert Carie sonne to the Lord Hunsdon,** Sir **Charles Blunt**, brother to the Lord Mountioy. But much speach is of two Gentlemen of the Court that went to the Nauie at the same time, whose names are **Thomas Gerard** and **William Heruie,** to me not knowen, but now here about London spoken of with great fame. These two aduentured out of ship boate, to scale the great Galliasse wherein Moncada was, and entred the same only with their Rapiers: a matter commonly spoken, that neuer the like was hazarded afore, considering the height of the Galliasse compared to a ship boate. And yet to make it more manifest, how earnest all sorts of Noble men, and Gentlemen, were to aduenture their liues in this seruice, it is reported that the **Earle of Oxford, who is one of the most auncient Earles of this land, went also to the Sea to serue in the Quéenes Army.** There went also for the same purpose, a second sonne of the Lord Treasurer, **called as I can remember, Robert Cecil** …

18 THE COPIE OF A LETTER

out knowledge of the Quéene, put themselues into the Quéens Nauy in sundry ships, wherein they serued at the fight afore Callice: of which number being very great, I remember that the names of some of them were these: Master Henry Brooke sonne & heire to the Lord Cobham, Sir Thomas Cecil sonne and heire to the Lord Treasurer, Sir William Hatton heire to the Lord Chancellour, Sir Horatio Pallauicino a Knight of Genua, Master Robert Carie sonne to the Lord Hunsdon, Sir Charles Blunt, brother to the Lord Mountioy. But much speach is of two Gentlemen of the Court that went to the Nauie at the same time, whose names are Thomas Gerard and William Heruie, to me not knowen, but now here about London spoken of with great fame. These two aduentured out of ship boate, to scale the great Galliasse wherein Moncada was, and entred the same only with their Rapiers: a matter commonly spoken, that neuer the like was hazarded afore, considering the height of the Galliasse compared to a ship boate.

Master Henry Brooke.
Sir Tho. Cecil.
Sir Wil. Hatton
Sir Horatio Pallauicino.
M. Robert Carie.
Sir Charles Blunt.
M. Thomas Gerard.
M. Wil. Heruie.

And yet to make it more manifest, how earnest all sorts of Noble men, and Gentlemen, were to aduenture their liues in this seruice, it is reported that the Earle of Oxford, who is one of the most auncient Earles of this land, went also to the Sea to serue in the Quéenes Army. There went also for the same purpose, a second sonne of the Lord Treasurer, called as I can remember, Robert Cecil: there went also about that time to

Earle of Oxford.
M. Robert Cecil.

List of English patriots who furnished ships

The "Mendoza letter" book immediately went to several editions and was translated into French. It seems odd that William Cecil would pretend to have trouble remembering his son Robert's name. However, the pretense is that this book was written in Spanish by an agent in England and was intercepted on its way to reach Ambassador Mendoza. Nelson (pp 314-315) notes that the original manuscript of the book is found to be entirely in Burghley's hand. Thus, we have direct evidence of Lord Burghley involved in a specific literary fraud. Nelson suggests that the feigned doubt over Robert Cecil's name was Burghley's way of hiding his connection to the text.

Notice how in the above quoted section, the honors go first to Henry Brooke, then Burghley's eldest, Thomas, and Sir William Hatton, third. Oxford is added as the ninth in this grouping. Perhaps Oxford bristled at this; a second "faux-Armada" book was published, in 1589, one that gives Oxford a higher ranking, and also contains so many anomalous qualities, that one is tempted to consider the pamphlet another de Vere creation.

This booklet (shown overleaf) was called:

> An Answer to the Untruthes, published and printed in Spaine, in glorie of their supposed victorie achieved against our English Navie, and the Right Honorable Charles, Lord Howard, Lord High Admiral of England &c., Sir Francis Drake, and the rest of the Nobles and Gentlemen, Captaines, and Soldiers of our said Navie.. First written in Spanish by a Spanish. ... Faithfully translated by I.L. Printed by John Jackson for Thomas Cadman, 1589.

Mr. "I.L." or "J.L." was, at one time attributed to John Lyly, but one of the interior poems is signed I. Lea. Neither a James or John Lea has ever been identified for this book. It is abundantly clear when reading the book that it was written in English and the entire framing device and claim of translation from a Spanish author is fraudulent. The book pretends to be a translation from a Spanish tract called, *Repvesta y Desengano contra las falsedades pulicades e impressas en Espana de la Armada Inglesa* by one "D.F.R. de. M.," allegedly a Spaniard left behind in England after the Armada. The Spanish language version was indeed published, but in England, by the same Thomas Cadman at the same time as the English version. Curiously, the Stationers' Register entry has an approval by Sir Francis Walsingham, the spymaster, making a highly unusual if not unique appearance in the Register.

There are many additional peculiarities to this publication:

- It opens with two dedication poems, one addressed to Queen Elizabeth, the other to Lord Admiral Howard. The Lord Admiral was a close friend of the Earl of Oxford. In the

AN ANSWER
TO THE VNTRVTHES, PVBLI-
SHED AND PRINTED IN SPAINE, IN
GLORIE OF THEIR SVPPOSED VICTORIE
atchieued againſt our Engliſh NAVIE, and the
Right Honorable CHARLES Lord HOWARD, Lord
high Admiral of England,&c.Sir FRANCIS DRAKE,
and the reſt of the Nobles and Gentlemen, Captaines,
and Soldiers of our ſaid Navie. First written and publiſhed in Spaniſh
By a Spaniſh

Gentleman; who came hither out of the Lowe
Countries from the ſeruice of the prince of PARMA,
with his wife and familie, ſince the overthrowe of
the Spaniſh Armado, forſaking both his countrie
and Romiſh religion; as by this Treatiſe(againſt
the barbarous impietie of the Spaniards;
and dedicated to the Queenes moſt
excellent Maieſtie) may
appeere.

Faithfully tranſlated by *I. L.*

LONDON,
Printed by Iohn Iackſon, for
Thomas Cadman.

1589.

An Answer to the Untruths, title page

May 1571 Tournament, Charles Howard and Oxford were among the challengers, when Thomas Bedingfield was on the defending team. In Oxford's letter of May 7, 1603, he refers to "...my Lord Admiral, my very good Lord and friend." At the close of the reign of Elizabeth, the only allowed theatrical companies were The Admiral's Men, The Lord Chamberlain's Men and the combined Oxford's Men-Worcester's Men troupe. Charles Howard and Edward de Vere had both been theatrical producers (though that term was not used) for decades. The prose dedication to Admiral Howard, which follows the opening poems in *An Answer to the Untruthes,* is entirely appropriate as he was the central hero of the Armada victory.

- Following the poems and dedication to the Admiral is a prose introduction to the Queen. The text begins by mentioning Saint Chrysostom. I have shown the significance of Chrysostom to Oxford in a previous paper, on the 1580 translation of Chrysostom's sermon on St. Paul's Epistle to the Ephesians that was published with a dedication to Anne Cecil de Vere, the Countess Oxford [See *Shakespeare Oxford Newsletter* Summer 2002]. The author then goes on a rant about the importance of Truth versus untruth and quotes Psalms 119 (printed in oversized letters) "Take not O Lord thy truth out of my mouth."

- The author works in the story of Pericles regarding Truth.

Pericles taught the same, when a certain friend requested him to affirm a lie for him and that with an oath, he answered him saying, It is lawful to be a friend, yet no farther than the altar." (*Untruthes,* p 8)

- The author mentions Holofernes. He also works in several odd experimental poems of assorted syllabic lengths and strange sarcastic songs. The author uses the metaphor of the echo to explain England's reasonable violence against Spain.

- While the alleged author is claimed to be a Spanish refugee soldier, this is a scholar's show-off book. While it may be too amateurish to have been written directly by the Earl of Oxford, I strongly suspect in came from his "studio" for lack of a better word. Lyly, may, indeed have been the ready penman, or even Angel Day, as it appeared in the window of Day's association with Oxford.

- The mention of Oxford comes during a long song of the Armada. "A song in praise of the English Nobility" (overleaf). In the relevant section, you will notice that the author has reversed and juggled the names of the volunteer nobles. Oxford, in ninth place in the William Cecil version, appears first in the corresponding section of *An Answer to the Untruthes:*

50 **An anſwer to certaine Spaniſh lies.**

Youths,deſirous of honor,and vſde the ſame to win,
do take their leave of friends,with many a brace & kiſſe,
From Father,from mother,from brothers,and from ſiſters,
from kindred,& from neighbors,& frō their houſhold chere:
They go towards the ſea,their enimies to ſeeke,
to die,or overcome,regarding life in little,
They go thinking upon war,and upon deeds of old
of their fathers,grandfathers,and others of their bloud,
They print in their memorie,the facts of their forefathers,
to ſhew themſelves no cowards,but bold,fierce,and ſtout,
And they,who thus do go are Gentle paſſing brave,
the Earles of Oxford,Northumberland,& Cumberlād,
Of valor,force,and courage,they beare the pricke and priſe,
three famous woorthy Earles,wel known and tried at armes,
Lord Dudley,Henry Brook,Arthur Gorge *and* Gerard,
which to aſſault & win,are fower woorthy ſoldiers,
The valorous Cicill,*which* Thomas *hath to name,*
who in affaires of wars,did never feare his foe,
Charles Blunt,William Hatton,*two ſoldiers noted well,*
Walter Rawleigh,*not the leaſt,nor uſed leſſe in armes,*
Robert Cicill,*and* William,*that is his brothers ſon,*
whoſe valor goes beyond,that of the wrathfull Mars,
Two famous Roberts *eeke,*Carie *and* Harvie *cald,*
of whome Fame proclaimes,affaires ſtrange and great:
Of Darcy *the valiant, whoſe name is called* Edward,

They go towards the sea, their enemies to seek,
To die, or overcome, regarding life in little,
They go thinking upon war and upon deeds of old,
Of their fathers, grandfathers, and others of their blood,
They print in their memories the facts of their forefathers,
To show themselves no cowards but bold, fierce, and stout,
And **they, who thus do go are Gentle passing brave,**
The Earles of Oxford, Northumberland, & Cumberland,
Of valor, force, and courage they bear the prick and prize
Three famous worthy Earls, well known and tried at arms,

Lord Dudley, Henry Brook, Arthur Gorge and Gerard
Which to assault and win are worthy soldiers
The valourous Cecill, which Thomas hathe to name
Who in affairs of wars did never fear his for,
Charles Blunt, William Hatton, two soldiers noted well,
Walter Raleigh, not the least nor used less in arms,
Robert Cecil and William, that is his brothers son,
whose valor goes beyond that of the wratful Mars.

Two famous Roberts eeke, Carie and Harvie cald,
Of whome fame proclaimes, affaires strange and great:
Of Darcy the valiant, whose name is Edward, …
(*Untruths,* page 50)

A few pages later we see:

What need I write of Brooke or Gorges praise
Of Hattons will of Dudleys skill in arms
Of Gerards hope, of Cecils haught affairs
Of Darcies power of Harvies hot alarms
Of Rawleighs art of Caries skill in lance
Of haught Horatio's stately check of chance

From foorth the Oxens tract to courtly State
I see the treasure of all science come
Whose pen of yore the muses style did mate
Whose sword is now unsheathed to follow drum
Parnassus knows my poet by his look
Charles Blunt, the pride of war and friend of booke.
(*Untruthes,* page 54)

M. Henrie Brooke.
M. Gorge.
Sir William Hatton.
L. Dudley.
M. Gerard.
Sir Thomas Cicill.
M. William Cicill.
M. Darcie.
M. R. Harvie.
Sir Walter Rawleigh.
M. Robart Carie.
*Oxford.
Sir Charles Blunt.

What neede I write of Brooke,*or* Gorges *praiſe,*
Of Hattons *will,of* Dudleys *skill in armes,*
Of Gerards *hope,of* Cicils *haught affaies,*
Of Darcies *power, of* Harvies *hot alarmes,*
Of Rawleighs *art, of* Caries *skill in lance:*
Of haught Horatios *ſtately checke of chance.*

From foorth the * Oxens *tract, to courtly ſtate,*
I ſee the treaſure of all Science come:
Whoſe pen of yore, the Muſes ſtile did mate,
Whoſe ſword is now unſheathd to follow drumbe,
Parnaſſus *knowes my Poet by his looke,*
Charles Blunt,*the pride of war and friend of booke.*

Some comments are required. Horatio, above, is Horatio Palacavino. The line about "the Oxens tract" has an asterisk in the original and a marginal note that simply says, "Oxford." While we may be led to assume that the school is referenced, because of "tract," the word appears to have been carefully chosen for its dual meaning. A tract is both a piece of land and a written account. ***"Whose pen of yore the muses style did mate."*** That can only refer to a poet. Spenser wrote of Oxford that he was beloved of the muses: "And also for the love which thou doest beare to th' Heliconian Ymps and they to thee" (Spenser's dedication to Oxford in the

Faerie Queene 1590). Day in *The English Secretary* 1586 wrote of Oxford, "the learned view and insight of your Lordship whose infancy from the beginning was ever sacred to the Muses."

Mt PARNASSUS _ CASTALIAN SPRING.

"Whose sword is now unsheathed to follow drum. Parnassus knows my poet by his look." Both these phrases remind us of Gabriel Harvey's earlier encomium to Oxford in which he rather boldly challenged the Earl to put down his pen and pick up his sword, and described him by the phrase, "Vultus Tela Vibrat," meaning, "Your **Look** Shakes Spears." Parnassus was the home of the muses.

The quick introduction of the name of Charles Blount, as a "friend of booke" may be a diversion, or may suggest he financed the book.

On the subject of "shaking spears," a variation of this allusion appears on another page of *Answer to the Untruthes,* in near juxtaposition to yet another verse on de Vere!

Here are the verses (reproduced at right):

Dictimne wakened by their bitter threats
Armed with her tools and weapons of defence
Shaking her lance, for inward passion sweats
Driving the thought of wonted peace from hence
And gliding through the circuit of the air
Unto Elias pallace did repair …

De-Vere whose fame, and loyalty hath pierced
The Tuscan clime and through the Belgike lands
By winged Fame for valor is rehearsed
Like warlike Mars upon the hatches stands
His tusked Bore gan foam for inward ire
While Pallas filled his breast with warlike fire.

Harvey's quip to Oxford, (Vultus Tela Vibrat) "Your look shakes spears," dates from 1579. This *Untruthes* material came ten years later, 1589. The first published work credited to "Shakespeare" was *Venus and Adonis,* 1593 On the title page, Parnassus is referenced by the allusion to the Castalian springs, the well of the Muses at Delphi on Mt. Parnassus.

53

*Dictimne, *wakened by their bitter threats:*
Armd with hir tooles, and weapons of defence:
Shaking hir launce, for inward passion, sweates,
Driving the thought of wonted peace from hence.
And gliding through the circute of the aire,
*Unto** Elisas *pallace did repaire.*

* The goddesse of war.

As when the flames amidst the fields of corne,
With hidious noise, awakes the sleepie swaine:
So do hir threatnings, seldome heard beforne,
Revive the warlike courtiers harts againe:
So foorth they presse, since Pallas *was their guide.*
And boldly saile upon the Ocean glide.

*Vnder the name of *Elisa* is ment, our gratious Queene Elizabeth.

The Admirall with Lion on his creast,
Like to Alcides *on the strond of Troy:*
Armd at assaie, to battell is addreast:
The sea that sawe his frownes, waxt calme and coy,
As when that Neptune *with threeforked mase,*
For Trojans sake, did keepe the winds in chase.

L. Admirall.

De-Vere *whose fame, and loyaltie hath pearst,*
The Tuscan *clime, and through the* Belgike *Lands,*
By winged Fame, for valor is rehearst:
Like warlike Mars *upon the hatches stands,*
His tusked Bore gan fome for inwarde ire,
While Pallas *fild his breast, with warlike fire.*

Earle of Oxford.

CHAPTER TWENTY SEVEN

The songs in *Daphnis and Chloe*

What may I call the sweete whence springs my sweetest ioy

What may I call the sweete whence springs my sweetest ioy,
Or wherein rests that on such sweete depends so great annoy.
How haps that where I touch the aire hath sweetest breath
And in the selfe-same fume I find my cause of death
Whence sues that where I liue where most delight I see
In selfe-same mood my life consumes, & ioies confounded bee
Whereon engendred is the heat that breeds the flame
Sith tempered is with sweetest blasts the cause that mooues the same
What phisicke may I finde what art to cure the sore,
Which guided by the aide it seekes the wound makes still the more.

Note: the joy/annoy rhyme; sith.

Sweete sweetned be the houres, the daies, the monthes and times

Sweete sweetned be **the houres, the daies, the monthes and times,**
Wherein with sweete conceipts my soule, thy sweetned fauor climes
Sweete be thy lookes, thy touch, thy speach, thy gate and all
Ten thousand sweets betide thee still, whose sweetnes staines them all.
Ye floures whose motlie hues do pranke in Natures pride.
Do shrowd your selues, and for my sweete, your beauties lay aside.
Ye temprate westerne winds, whose aire yeilds sweetned breath
Denie your sweete to be as hers, whose sweet yeelds life or death
Ye deintie tuned fowles whose notes do decke the spring
Confesse in hearing of her soundes, your sweets small pleasure bring
Ye christall sacred springs, ye vales and mountaines hie,
Whose pleasant walkes her passage decks, and spreading fauours die
Agree with me in this, my sweete (surpassing far)
Excels the sweetnes of you all, and doth your pleasures bar.

Compare with Shakespeare's Sonnet LVII:

Being your slave what should I do but tend
Upon **the hours, and times** of your desire?
I have no precious time at all to spend;
Nor services to do, till you require.
Nor dare I chide the world without end hour,
Whilst I, my sovereign, watch the clock for you,
Nor think the bitterness of absence sour,
When you have bid your servant once adieu;
Nor dare I question with my jealous thought
Where you may be, or your affairs suppose,
But, like a sad slave, stay and think of nought
Save, where you are, how happy you make those.
  So true a fool is love, that in your will,
  Though you do anything, he thinks no ill.

Those hears the golden wiers of my wel tuned sounde

Those hears the golden wiers of my wel tuned sounde,
Become the pleasure of my panges, and make my ioyes abounde.
These seemely eies the glasse, whereof my fewture staies,
And forehead large, the field on which, depends my blisfull raies.
This mouth the deintie spring, that yeldes me cause of life,
These teeth the pearles of precious price, that cure mine inward grife.
These lips the curroll fresh, that comforts heart and mind,
These looks the guarders of my loue, by whom I fauor find,
Those cheeks the apples fresh, whereon Vermilion taint,
Be mixed with the siluer white, my sugred pleasure paint.
These pits in dented cheeks, are chaires for Beautie plaste,
Wherein, triumphant fauor sits, impugning woes to waste.
This necke of yu'ry white, confounder of my cares,
These hands the aids to further that, which loue for me prepares.
These feet the wished steps, whereout my ioies arise
From these and out of these ensue, what els I may deuise.
Thus decked in my ioyes, on her I gaze my fil
Whose shape hath power to comfort all, but neuer force to spill

To thee thou winged God, what ere thou bee

To thee thou winged God, what ere thou bee
(A god thou art) we sheepheards fruits do bring
Let Daphnis and his heards be deare to thee,
And Chloes flocks eft cast this sacred spring.

Ye brightest gleames within those percing eies

Daphnis Ye brightest gleames within those percing eies
Whose glimpse retaines a shew of power deuine
Enclose your selues, for feare from loftie skies
Some enuious star do at your glory pine.

Chloe Ye mightie powers, to whom these sacred groues
Right pleasing bene. And Nimphes that haunt this shade,
Enuie you not with wreake the hardye proues
That Natures selfe in Daphnis shape hath made

Daphnis Alas if Phœbus should the heat for-thinke
That once for loue in burning breast he bare
And mazed at thy fewter, gin to shrincke
From her to thee, then woe betide my share.

Chloe Alas if Venus stealing to her springs
In mind her sweet Adonis to embrace
Thy curled locks should vew whose beautie stings
And thee for him admire, then woe my case.

Daphnis Excelling iewels, beare the choisest price
Things lesse in shewe, enuie alwaies the best:
Lesse Phœbe shines, when Tytan ginnes to rise
Where mightie force effects, there shrowds the least.

Chloe Unmatched pearles, haue value still for showe
When best exceeds, who can denie the place
Though things be rated hie, yet this we knowe
It (needs) excels, whose weight hath highest grace.

Daphnis Be honored then, thou Nimphe of all the flockes

Chloe Be fairest thou of all that guide their heard

Daphnis Let still thy name resound on hiest rockes

Chloe And Chloe ne're be of thy chaunge afeard.

To love alas, what may I call this loue?

To loue alas, what may I call this loue?
This vncouth loue, this passion wondrous straunge,
A mischiefe deadlie, such as for to proue
My heart would shunne, if powre I had to chaunge.

To chaunge said I? recant againe that sownd
Recant I must, recant it shall indeed
Sith in my heart so many things abound
As yeelds desert how ere my fancies speede.
Sweete is the lure that feeds my gazing eies
Sweete be the lookes, that whet my hot desire
Sweete is the harbour where my quiet'lies
But to vnsweete, the meanes for to aspire.
Yet must I loue? I must, and so I doe.
Suppoze it hard the thing whereat I reach
Who doubtes but pearles are for the best to wooe
And greatest mindes to highest actions stretch.
Be witnes yet (my flockes) of all my paine
And sacred groues that knowe my iust complaint
Let aie my loue within this barke remaine
Whom harmefull force haue neuer power to taint.

What griefe alas, what hell vnto my woes?

What griefe alas, what hell vnto my woes?
What sorrow may exceede my foule mishap?
What more excesse than mischiefe where it flowes?
Or deepe dispaire that all my woes doeth wrap?
Vnhappy downes, what ailed wicked spight
To reaue from you and me, our sweete delight.
My tender kiddes if ere your louing skips
You beare in minde, and on this pleasant dale
How manie times your young delightfull trips
Haue Daphnis mo'ud to mourne his bitter bale
Then for his sake that whilom was your guide
Yeeld foorth your plaints, and griefes to you betide.
Ye mournefull flockes dispersed where ye goe
To vncouth pastures yeeld my drearie tunes
Lamenting teares, and sighings full of woe
Wherein my thoughts for Chloes loue consumes
Let be your foode, and your tender walkes
Conceiue the sorrowe that my pleasure balkes
Returne to me your stately beards
Returne My heart, my ioye, my comfort and my care,
My blisfull Chloe once againe returne.
Ye sacred Nymphs, or death for me prepare
Seale vp your springs, and praise in secret lie
If Chloes rape doe cause her Daphnis die.

Compare with Oxford's poem:

What plague is greater than the grief of mind?
The grief of mind that eats in every vein;
In every vein that leaves such clots behind;
Such clots behind as breed such bitter pain;
So bitter pain that none shall ever find,
What plague is greater than the grief of mind.

Ye heauens (if heauens haue power to iudge of things amisse)

Ye heauens (if heauens haue power to iudge of things amisse)
Ye earthlie guides that swaie and rule, the stem of all my blisse,
Ye starres if you can iudge, ye Planets if ye knowe
Of haynous wrongs, that tendred beene to men on earth belowe,
Then iudge, repute, & deeme, giue sentence and diuine
Of all the wo that rues my hart, and causlesse makes me pine,
If right to men of right belongs with equall doome,
Then heauens I pray admit my teares, and do my plaints resume,
Your sacred powre it is that yeeldes me bale or boote:
The sighs I spend are else but waste, and vaine is all my sute.
I loue, alas, I loue, and loued long I haue,
My loue to labour turned is, my hope vnto the graue,
My fruit is time mispent, mispending breedes my gaine,
My gaine is ouer-rulde by losse, and losse breedes all my paine,
Here my gastly ghost could halt or go awrie,
I aske no fauour for my sute, but let me starue and die,
But if by fixed faith by trouth I sought to clime
By seruice long that nere should be shut vp by any time.
Yf onely zeale I beare to that I most desire
And choice reguard of purest thoughts hath set my heart on fire
Why should not my reward conformed be with those
Whose liues at happiest rate are led and craue aright suppose
If this be all I seeke, if sole for this I serue
Then heauens vouchsafe to graunt me this els let me die and sterue.

CHAPTER TWENTY EIGHT

Prior Oxfordian scholarship on *The English Secretary*

WHILE I AM NOT the first Oxfordian to discuss Angel Day and *The English Secretary*, this is the first in-depth study of Day's work in an Oxfordian context (or in any context.) But I must acknowledge the prior work on this subject by researchers and writers who have preceded me.

John Thomas Looney, in *Shakespeare Identified*, 1920, the first full-length Oxfordian proposal, does not mention Angel Day or his books.

B. M. Ward's *Seventeenth Earl of Oxford*, 1928, has a brief mention of Day in the context of the 1586 dedication to Oxford in the first edition of *The English Secretary.*

Dorothy and Charlton Ogburn Sr.'s *This Star of England*, 1952, offers a few brief mentions of Day's *English Secretary*, giving a pull quote from the 1586 dedication and describing Oxford as a patron to Day, without specifics.

Ruth Loyd Miller's *Oxfordian Vistas*, 1975, mentions the 1586 edition of *The English Secretary* in her detailed chronology of Oxford's life. In her overall index, she describes Angel Day as a "retainer of Oxford" without elaboration.

Charlton Ogburn Jr.'s *The Mysterious William Shakespeare*, 1984, on page 688, offers a single pull quote from the 1586 dedication, as demonstrative of Oxford's standing as a patron to many young authors in the 1580s.

Katherine Chiljan's *Dedication Letters to The Earl of Oxford*, 1994, offered readers the first short explanation, in context, of Day's epistles to Oxford, and she reproduced entirely both the 1586 dedication and the 1599 dedication to Oxford, from the first and fourth editions of *The English Secretary.*

Alan Nelson, in *Monstrous Adversary,* 2003, mentions Angel Day's 1586 dedication to Oxford, and even quotes, "whose infancy from the beginning was ever sacred to the Muses."

Mark K. Anderson, in *Shakespeare By Another Name,* 2005, gives Angel Day a fuller treatment than those before. He also credits Sarah Smith, in an unpublished paper, with an insight into the faux-Bowes letter included in the 1586 *English Secretary.* I've now read Ms. Smith's short essay, which was presented at an academic conference.

Bibliography

Arber, Edward, ed., *Transcript of the Registers of the Company of Stationers of London* (London 1875)

Anderson, Mark, *Shakespeare by Another Name,* New York, 2005

Andrews, Michael Cameron, "His mother's Closet: A note on Hamlet" in *Modern Philology* November 1982

Arte of English Poesie (1589)

Ashcom, B.B., "Notes on the Development of the Scanderbeg Theme," *Comparative Literature 5,* 1 (Winter 1953)

Austin, Warren B., "Angel Day", article in *Notes and Queries,* Nov. 12, 1938

Bellot, Hugh, *The Inner and Middle Temple,* London, 1902

Brassington, William Salt, *Shakespeare's Homeland,* London, 1903

British Rhetoricians and Logicians 1500-1660, *Dictionary of Literary Biography,* Volume 236, 2001

Cerasano, S.P., "Day, Angell" (fl. 1563–1595), *Oxford Dictionary of National Biography,* Oxford University Press, 2004

Cecil, Robert, "The State and Dignity of a Secretary of State's Place, with the Care and Peril Thereof," in *The Harleian Miscellany 5* (1810): 166-68

Day, Angel, *The English Secretorie. Wherein is contayned, A Perfect Method...*(London 1586).

Day, Angel, *The English Secretorie: or plaine and direct Method...* (London 1592/93).

Day, Angel, *The English Secretorie: or plaine and direct Method...* (London 1595).

Day, Angel, *The English Secretary, or Methode of writing of Epistles and Letters...* (London 1599).

Evans, Robert O., *The English Secretary* or, Methods of writing epistles and letters; with, A declaration of such tropes, figures, and schemes, as either usually or for ornament sake are therein required. (1599) A facsimile reproduction, with an introd., by Robert O. Evans; Gainesville, Fla., Scholars' Facsimiles & Reprints, 1967.

Gillespie, Stuart, *Shakespeare's Books,* Continuum, 2001

Goldberg, Jonathan, *Writing Matter: From the Hands of the English Renaissance* (Stanford:

Stanford Univ. Press, 1990).

Hildebrandt, Herbert W., "A 16th Century Work on Communication: Precursor of Modern Business Communication," Working Paper #190, Division of Research, Graduate School of Business Administration, University of Michigan, 1979

Hornbeak, Katherine Gee, "The Complete Letter-Writer in English, 1500-1800," *Smith College Studies in Modern Languages 15* (1934)

Jones, William J., "Due Process and Slow Process in the Elizabethan Chancery" in *American Journal of Legal History,* 1962, [Vol. 6 #2]

Kinney, Arthur F., *Humanist Poetics, thought, rhetoric, and fiction in 16th century England,* U Mass Press, 1986

Magnusson, Lynne, *Shakespeare and Social Dialogue: Dramatic language and Elizabethan Letters,* Cambridge University Press, 1999.

McManaway, James G., An uncollected poem of John Skelton, *Notes and Queries,* March 31, 1951

Nelson, Alan, *Monstrous Adversary,* Liverpool University Press, 2003

Nicholl, Charles, *A Cup of Newes, The Life of Thomas Nashe,* London 1984

Nicholl, Charles, *The Reckoning, The Murder of Christopher Marlowe,* London 1992

Oxford English Dictionary (OED), Oxford 1933, reprint 1970

Panek, Jennifer, *Widows and Suitors in early Modern English Comedy,* Cambridge University Press, 2004

Parker, Patricia "Othello and Hamlet" in *Shakespeare Reread: The texts in New Contexts,* Ross McDonald, ed., Ithaca, NY, 1994

Plant, Marjorie, *The English Book Trade,* London, 1939, pp. 131-139.

Rambuss, Richard, "The Secretary's Study: The Secret designs of The Shepheardes Calender" *English Literary History 59* (1992) pp 313-335.

Robertson, Jean, "Angel Day," article in *Notes & Queries,* August 13, 1938

Robertson, Jean, *The Art of Letter Writing; An Essay On Handbooks published in England During the Sixteenth and Seventeenth Centuries* (London: Univ. Press of Liverpool, 1942)

Schoenbaum, Samuel, *William Shakespeare, A Documentary Life,* NY 1975

Scofield, Martin, "Shakespeare and Clarissa," in *Shakespeare Survey 51* (1998)

Shakespeare, *The Winter's Tale,* Arden edition edited by J.H.P. Pafford, 1963, 1986

Sixteenth century non-dramatic writers, *Dictionary of Literary Biography* Volume 167, Third Series 1996

Simmons, J. L., "Holland's Pliny and Troilus and Cressida" in *Shakespeare Quarterly* (v27.3, Summer 1976)

Stritmatter, Roger, "The Marginalia of Edward de Vere's Geneva Bible" Dissertation, UMass 2001, Oxenford Press, Northampton, MA

Wolff, Luella M., "A Brief History of the Art of Dictamen: Medievel Origins of Business Letter Writing., *Journal of Business Communication 16,* No. 2 (Winter 1979)

Index

www.ingramcontent.com/pod-product-compliance
Lightning Source LLC
LaVergne TN
LVHW020718110826
845149LV00012B/2323

* 9 7 8 0 9 8 5 3 9 3 8 1 6 *